"Why do we make the Gospel academic a[...] honest, warm, and real? Why do we make [...] life he was so inviting? Why do we make the message a moral contest instead of a mystical encounter? Well, this fine book will make none of those mistakes. Linda Rooney offers you positive, faith-filled, and mature Christianity."

**Richard Rohr, O.F.M.**
Center for Action and Contemplation

"*Walking the Disciple's Path* inspires, challenges, and leads the reader through prayerful reflection on God's word. This interactive work leads to transformation, not just of oneself, but of one's surroundings."

**Most Reverend Robert F. Morneau**
Auxiliary Bishop of the Diocese of Green Bay

"Linda Rooney has created a rich spiritual book that will nourish the journey of those just beginning their spiritual walk as well as those who have been on the road for a while. The reader will find considerable substance woven in a variety of strands including life story, scripture, poetry, and imagery. Rooney's methods will engage the reader's heart and open it to a deeper understanding and experience of God's gracious love and ongoing call."

**Maureen A. Kelly**
Author of *Christian Initiation*

"*In Walking the Disciple's Path*, Linda Rooney has provided us with a road map for the modern spiritual life. This book is loaded with practical advice and challenging principles, a step-by-step guide to understanding and growing in our intimacy with Christ. It reads like a 'journal for the soul.' I'd like to put it into the hands of anyone who ever doubted or desired greater faith."

**Bill Huebsch**
PastoralPlanning.com

"*Walking the Disciple's Path* provides an excellent guide for anyone attempting to discern how God is calling him or her as a disciple. Rooney breaks open familiar gospel passages in a way that helps the reader see the relationship of the passages to everyday, ordinary life. She assists the reader in developing a deeper, more personal relationship with their God and directs the disciple to ways of living this relationship. She helps our 'hearts respond to our reflections' in ways that lead to action."

**Loughlan Sofield, S.T.**
Coauthor of *Principled Ministry*

"Woven in faith and love and rich with wit and wisdom, *Walking the Disciple's Path* invites us to reawaken our religious imagination to explore the Gospels in deeper and more meaningful ways. Linda Rooney invites us into this experience with meditations, personal stories, thoughtful reflection questions, and creative rituals. Each of her eight steps challenge and inspire us to experience Jesus and his message as if for the first time. This is the perfect book for those seeking to embrace the Gospel message, but just don't know where to begin."

**Gwen Costello**
Author of *Blessed Are You*

"*Walking the Disciple's Path* is an invaluable must-read. Linda Rooney's eight steps are practical, pastoral, and spiritually based—a godsend to those who are active in life and ministry and need specific suggestions to live an integrated life. Rooney roots her reflections in the stories of Jesus and those of ordinary people whom she has come to admire and love. She is a great storyteller, rich in imagery and imagination, encouraging her readers to claim the gospel dynamics—the good news of their own lives."

**Ed Sellner**
Author of *Finding the Monk Within*

"Linda Rooney takes biblical passages, expands them, and challenges us to imagine what it was like then and what it means for us today. She gives us the opportunity to look at our choices, at what we hold in our hearts and what we do in our lives, and to consider how those choices align with our invitation to love."

**Lynn Durham**
Author of *From Frazzled to Fantastic!*

# WALKING THE DISCIPLE'S PATH

Eight Steps That Will
Change Your Life
and the World

## Linda Perrone Rooney

ave maria press AMP notre dame, indiana

Founded in 1865, Ave Maria Press is a ministry of the United States Province of Holy Cross.

www.avemariapress.com

Paperback: ISBN-10 1-59471-368-5, ISBN-13 978-1-59471-368-2

E-book: ISBN-10 1-59471-369-3, ISBN-13 978-1-59471-369-9

Cover image © Thinkstock.

Cover and text design by Katherine Robinson.

Printed and bound in the United States of America.

*Library of Congress Cataloging-in-Publication Data*

Rooney, Linda Perrone.

 Walking the disciple's path : eight steps that will change your life and the world / Linda Perrone Rooney.

  pages cm

 ISBN 978-1-59471-368-2 (pbk.) -- ISBN 1-59471-368-5 (pbk.)

 1. Christian life--Catholic authors. I. Title.

 BX2350.3.R66 2013

 248.4--dc23

                           2012046443

# CONTENTS

# INTRODUCTION

When I was a little girl, spirituality was not a word that tripped easily off the lips of the Catholic community into which I was born and raised. I daresay it wasn't used much among Christians in general. In those days, God was mediated to us through our religion, and it was thought that in learning our "religion" we would meet the living God. Symbols, religious imagination, and devotions were also held in great esteem. And this was good. It was common to see numerous statues in church, reminders of those who had gone before us, whose faith was so much greater than ours could ever be. Likewise, what we now call "smells and bells" were everywhere. Incense was a regular part of the ceremony of Sunday Mass, not an occasional "treat." Bells sounding at the consecration, processions, draped statues during Lent, genuflecting, kneeling, and chant in a language we didn't understand but still felt swept up in were all ways in which our religious imaginations were triggered and enriched. And it was good.

Yet with all the emphasis on the external, the core of our faith, scripture, wasn't emphasized. If anything, it was de-emphasized among the laity because our Protestant brothers and sisters lived by "sola scriptura" and Martin Luther had not yet been forgiven. We prayed our rosaries at Mass, not realizing the incongruity in giving more attention to our "beads" than to the bread and wine. Rosaries, novenas, prayers on the backs of holy cards, and favorite saints each had their place in drawing us into the embrace of God's presence. I loved it even while I didn't know what else I was missing. I never imagined that any other type of religious experience could capture my attention or bring me so close to God.

I attended a Catholic elementary school and an all-girl Catholic high school, and was surrounded by Catholic friends, teachers, and family members. But always, even within this cocoon of a safe and unchanging religious environment, God was working within me. I acknowledged my personal relationship with God at the age of seven, and I distinctly remember the first time I understood that this relationship would not only bring peace to but also challenge my orderly and safe world.

The challenge to understand began early: I was ten and sitting in a front-row seat in my fifth-grade classroom. Our religion teacher, a Sister, told us that anyone who did not go to Mass on Sunday would go to hell—no questions and no exceptions—which was a pre–Vatican II thought. The intellectual part of me that was accustomed to believing everything she said about God believed her. But another part of me felt unsettled and began to question. My heart brought me thoughts of my dad, who seldom went to Mass and whom I loved very much. "Sister," I asked, "what if a person is very good to everyone, believes in God, and does good things in his life? Won't God forgive him for missing Mass?" "No," she said. Seeing the look on her face, I swallowed my next thoughts, but they didn't go away. All that day and evening, I thought about how I could get my dad to go to Mass so that he could avoid hell. During the night, I woke up crying. There was a small Infant of Prague statue, given to me at my first Communion, sitting on my dresser, and seeing it, I was moved to pray. I asked God to tell me what to do to save my father. I don't remember the words, just the experience. That night I learned to trust in God's mercy and love, to not judge my father, and to remember that each relationship with God was a mystery that couldn't be unraveled with rules and laws, as good as they might be. I heard God ask me to love my dad and to show him by my own actions that church meant something important and he was missing it.

My young soul recognized the truth of this experience. It changed forever the way in which I heard my religion lessons. It opened my mind and my heart to questions that have no fixed answers, except trust in God's love and mercy. It allowed me to find peace within the scope of the mysteries of life as they unfolded in my life.

My love for and relationship with my dad opened me to understand how great God's love is. And learning the truth of God's love transformed my life, though I did not know then how it would shape me.

When I found myself writing, I knew that I had to write about certain themes: God's love and mercy; healing; the struggle to live as a disciple of Christ; the joy that comes when we are able to offer a faithful response to the love God pours out; and the spiritual life. My writing seems naturally to revolve around these themes because I find them woven into the fabric of my life as well as within the lives of my friends, family, students, and clients in counseling and spiritual direction. Daily I listen to the stories that others share with me, of faith seeking understanding, and they resonate in my own soul. It is these stories that have taught me what most of us seek when we seek God.

We seek mercy, unconditional love, assurance that God has not forgotten us, assistance with the task of meeting life's problems with grace and dignity, strength to be faithful to our commitments, knowledge of God through the Church's teaching, reconciliation with others and within ourselves, and so much more. We seek a personal and sustaining relationship with a God who loves us.

I read a book once that mentioned an old saying: "Facts can explain us, but only story will save us." If you want to destroy a person, nation, or religion, destroy their stories. If you want to empower others, give them a story to share. This is what God has done for us, and it is one of the treasures of our Christian-Catholic faith. Our God gave us a story of creative and unconditional love that is imprinted on creation, and especially on the spirit of human beings. Our Jewish ancestors in faith shared this timeless, rich story of God's love and of how precious we are in God's sight in the Hebrew scriptures, where we find God's abiding presence, protection, and graciousness in good times and bad. The story continued with the Incarnation of Jesus, whose coming among us gave dignity to our humanity. Our spiritual story has its heroes and heroines, and we continue to write it each day that we live.

In *Walking the Disciple's Path*, I have tried to share the great story of God's love and mercy by appealing to our religious imagination—that wondrous, mystical reality so appealingly displayed in times gone by, especially in the writings and lives of the saints. I've used scripture, our first source of God's story; poetry; imaginative meditations; personal stories; rituals; and thoughtful reflection questions to provide a variety of ways through which the Spirit residing in you and seeking to guide your life can be tapped into and exposed. In essence, this book is an introduction to moving from the head to the heart.

For some, this approach may be a new way of reading scripture, but it has been a cherished tradition for the Church for centuries. Monasteries used lectio divina to help monks apply the scriptures to their everyday lives. St. Francis of Assisi's creative imagining of scripture inspired people to create nativity scenes at Christmas and to imagine the Holy Family as people like us. Four hundred years later, St. Ignatius of Loyola used imaginative scriptural reflection as a key part of his life-transforming Spiritual Exercises. This is the tradition in which I was raised and educated and that I'm sharing with you.

In *Walking the Disciple's Path*, we will follow that ancient tradition of placing ourselves within the scene and noticing what is around us, who else is there, and what we see and hear. We will imagine the conversations, the mood. Scripture reading, in this way, is an avenue toward prayer, not a study manual. It engages us in relationship with the characters in the sacred story and allows us to identify with them and to resonate with the possibilities inherent in the life of Jesus. We use our *minds* to access thinking and reflection, but it is how our *hearts* respond to our reflection that will lead us to conversion and *action*. That's what happened to me as I prayed in the middle of the night. My mind was filled with thoughts that were sifted through my heart and my love for my dad. The truth that emerged for me inspired my own commitment to attend Mass each week out of love not fear and to let my choices speak to my dad as a witness.

Each page of this book was written in faith and love, and is as rich as any tapestry with the wit and wisdom of the people that populate my life. It was written for seekers who agree that we are always on a journey to deeper understanding of and relationship with our God. Its message will comfort and challenge, inspire and stimulate. I hope that it will ignite or reignite that love affair with God, in Christ, that their Spirit has been fomenting in you, dear reader, all of your life.

I offer you this book with a deep appreciation for the journey you are about to take. It is a journey that incorporates basic teachings about faith, and may be the most challenging steps you will take in your walk with Christ. I walk the journey with you, in hope and in the assurance given in the gospel stories and confirmed by my lived experience that our lives will be richer, more serene, and more Christ-like because we have stepped out and followed the disciple's path. Through us, our world will be brought into union with God.

May your reading of this book inspire your faith, challenge your spirit, and lead your faith from your head to your heart so that, as a disciple, you will shine with incredible acts of service and love. Keep in mind,

> God is with us.
> *God*
> Is with us
> In creation,
> In Jesus,
> In the Holy Spirit,
> In each other,
> In the Eucharist,
> In signs and wonders,
> In disasters and tragedies
> In war and peace
> In life and death;
> Within
> Outside
> Around
> Up, Under, and Over,
> GOD IS WITH US!

# Surrender
# Your
# Nets

As he walked by the Sea of Galilee, he saw two brothers, Simon, who is called Peter, and Andrew his brother, casting a net into the sea—for they were fishermen. And he said to them, "Follow me and I will make you fishers of [men]." Immediately they left their nets and followed him. As he went from there he saw two other brothers, James, son of Zebedee and his brother, John, in the boat with their father, Zebedee, mending their nets and he called them. Immediately they left the boat and their father and followed him.

Matthew 4:18–22

1

## Imagine and Reflect

Who are these men who spend their lives fishing,
Rough and smelly,
Always tired from battling the sea?
Experts they are at catching fish,
Providing for their families,
Searching the sea for what avoids being found.
The sea is all they know.
This casting of nets is what they do best.
It forms their identities; it is their comfort.
But when the stranger calls them
To walk, without fear, into His embrace,
They leave their nets, change their hearts,
And enter new waters teeming with those waiting to be
found.

## Fishing in the Everydayness of Life

Christians have heard this scripture about "fishing for men" since childhood. The picturesque scene appeals to our imaginations. Traditionally, this passage was used to support the teaching that the Twelve were lowly and humble men whom Jesus called to be his apostles and, thus, leaders of his Church. That teaching emphasized their leadership and the ultimate cultic priesthood that evolved historically. But is that all there is to the story? What does that story say to us as twenty-first-century men and women?

As I mentioned in the introduction, this book was written to assist us in connecting scripture to our lives, offering a way to recognize and answer our own call to follow Christ. Now, in this first chapter, as we begin to engage the invitation given to the fishermen by Jesus, we realize that their call is directed at our own lives as well. As those baptized into the life of Christ, the waters we are called to fish are found in our everyday circumstances. It is here that the "fish" wait to be found by Christ, through us. What does it mean to become "fishers of men"? In a faith sense, becoming a "fisherman" is akin to proclaiming the good news, witnessing by word and example that Christ is our Savior. The Great Commission to "go and make disciples" is what we are called, by baptism, to do. We disciples are sent to call others, to make new disciples.

However, before we can accept Christ's invitation to follow him and evangelize, we have to understand what it means. The journey through this book offers clues to harnessing spiritual wisdom so that we can accomplish the task of witnessing to our faith. Our baptismal calling, the words of scripture, and the life of the Church all equip us to become and make disciples using our own rod of faith and net of good works.

## Entering the Scripture Story: Ordinary People

As we imagine Matthew's seaside account of the call of the fishermen, we see that the fishermen were ordinary people. Like us, they went about their daily task of earning a living. They also share several characteristics with us: their lives depend on their best efforts; they work hard both alone and together with others; they understand their environment and how it affects their goals; they have courage and take risks; and finally, they use the resources at their disposal to accomplish the day's work. Each of these characteristics deserves additional reflection as we deepen our appreciation of how these aspects of their lives apply to our own lives and relationships with Christ.

### These are not wealthy men or people of influence

Our fishermen lived in first-century Palestine. They come from families who have worked the sea, farmed, or been craftsmen for generations. They take pride in doing their trade well. Calling them ordinary might be misleading because it could be interpreted to mean that what they do isn't important or that who they are and what they have to offer isn't unique or significant enough. But only a foolish person would dismiss those who are considered ordinary. Wasn't it the Son of God who was born in an ordinary stable, to an ordinary man and woman?

We live in a society that elevates wealth, prestige, popularity, and public figures to such a degree that those not singled out might see their lives as less valuable or less important. Perhaps, like me, you have felt this way at times. By choosing ordinary people, Christ shows us that every life can be used to witness to him and to change the world.

### They are laborers

These men support their families by the sweat of their brows, and their hard work is marked by the calluses on their hands, by what they catch and sell each day. If they don't work, they don't eat, nor do their families. The family is one of the four cornerstones of Jewish life, and no good Jew would ignore his responsibilities to his family. Each day was a day to wrestle with survival, and it is in this struggle to hold fast to our beliefs, traditions, and values in the face of constant difficulties that the uniqueness and sacredness of the ordinary manifests itself.

When I walked near the Sea of Galilee, I was touched by the realization that on that same shore Jesus strolled in search of companions to walk with him as his disciples. It dawned on me that where God calls me to be is right where I am, doing those things that I am gifted to do and trying to be faithful to the relationships that are part of my life. Our work, our families, and our values are not trivial appendages to some greater call. They are the sacred environments in which we are meant to meet Christ and to learn the purpose of our lives.

### Fishermen understand their environment

Peter and the others knew which fish were best to catch in which season, whether the skies spoke of safety or peril, how best to work together to enhance the total fish take, and who in the village would buy their catch. They believed that God, the giver of all good things, was with them. They lived by the sea and took sustenance from its depths for all of their lives. Their history with the sea and with God taught them that God provides if they are willing to do their part, to do what is necessary to find and catch the fish. Their hope for the future was colored by their memory of God's providence in the past. They went out in safe or dangerous weather because experience taught them that different circumstances demand different approaches and in every situation they were in God's care. These attitudes are not unique to these particular fishermen; they are attitudes that form their whole culture and permeate the world in which they live. These values are rooted in the lived faith of their religion and their ancestors.

We each live in a set of unique circumstances that include urban, suburban, and rural elements; differing ethnic and religious backgrounds; a distinctive set of family of origin traditions, expectations, and experiences; and a particular way of seeing and understanding the world. This truth comes home to me whenever I give a talk in any part of the country. After the introductions, I ask if anyone in the audience has any connection to western New York. Inevitably, someone does, and we joke about the idiosyncratic memories we share. I immediately feel at home, and my new friends always come up afterward to share with "one of their own." Our environments have formed who we are and how we view the world, and through them, Christ seeks us out and issues our call.

### Fishermen take risks

They aren't scared off by a little rain. They go out into the deep of the sea, beyond what their natural fears and caution might indicate is best, in order to find a catch that makes their labors meaningful. They are not reckless—but they are courageous, realizing that if they allow their fears to guide their judgment, nothing of worth will be accomplished. The support they give each other minimizes what might make an individual man fearful. Together, they have learned that they need each other and can depend on each other. They know and believe what God taught in the Torah: be not afraid.

So often fear is the reason we don't step out to achieve the purpose of our lives. We fear failure, criticism, rejection, and so much more. When I first started writing for publication, I encountered this fear, and for quite some time I hesitated to show anyone my work. Yet, like the fishermen, eventually I had to make a choice to step out of my zone of comfort. Those who follow Christ are called to make a difference in the world. We do not have the luxury of giving in to our fears. As did the fishermen, we can choose to go beyond our fears in order to learn and fulfill the purpose for which God placed us on this earth.

### Fishermen are adept at using the tools of their trade

Every first-time fisherman starts with a simple fishing pole, and I imagine our scriptural fishermen were no different. However, born into this tradition, they quickly learned that a single fishing line needed to give way to a net because the sea in which they fished was too quickly deep and too wildly unpredictable to use only a single fish line. Nets bring a larger catch in a shorter period of time. While the nets are unwieldy for solitary fishing, a team of men can handle both the boat and the nets with success and safety. Their teamwork in the past taught them the value of relying on each other and on each one's abilities to achieve the desired results.

The nets work for the men, but the men take care of their nets, as James and John were doing when Jesus came. On off days, rainy days, and days when the sea is too dangerous, the fishermen tend to their nets, mending those that are torn, lengthening and strengthening where needed, and examining each and every link to be sure that, when the catch is ready, so are the nets. They also dispose of those nets that no longer are helpful to them, those that are torn beyond repair or weakened to the point of danger. They are wise in discerning which nets to use and when a net is no longer helpful.

Just as we do spring cleaning and sort what is no longer of use, following Christ involves a regular appraisal of what is helping or hindering our spiritual journey. Baptism is only the beginning of the real work of being a disciple. It takes a lifetime to realize how to integrate what we believe with what we do, and how to maintain a spiritual relationship with Christ that consistently is seen in the choices we make and the lives we live.

Like the fishermen called from their nets to follow Christ, we, too, don't always recognize him as he first approaches. He looks like everyone else, and we meet him within the circumstances we have come to believe are "ordinary." There are no trumpets sounding or colors flashing as Christ approaches, and yet, our hearts know that something is different. What are the signs of this difference?

When Christ is present, we recognize a desire to reach out to help someone; we experience a sense of guilt for making choices that are neither healthy nor in sync with our best selves; and we are aware of a yearning for inner peace and a willingness to forgive. These, and others, are signs of Christ's call to become like him, and like the fishermen, intuitively we realize that in order to answer something will need to change. As we continue to enter this vocational story and to imagine it from the perspective of the encounter between Jesus and the fishermen, we'll learn more of what this change, this conversion, will involve.

## Listening From the Heart:
## The Beginning of Conversion

In the introduction, I mentioned the Church's rich tradition of using an imaginative approach to reflecting on scripture. Here we begin that process. I invite you to let your mind rest awhile and to allow your imagination to see the vast sea, the men at work with their nets; to smell the ocean and the fish; to visualize the scene; and to allow yourself to enter it as I guide you along.

These are real people. What might they have been thinking and feeling? We are given only a Spartan glimpse in the scripture passage. Surely more happened. What might it have been like? What can we learn about how God works in our own lives, not just in the lives of these scriptural characters? Enter with trust that the Spirit is guiding us into deeper relationship with Christ as has happened throughout history when men and women of faith have wrestled with how to understand the meaning of the sacred story for their own lives.

## The Call

As we enter the story of the call of the first disciples, visualize a man walking along the seashore who stops to notice the teamwork, strength, and energy of a group of fishermen, and their dedication to what they are about. While still distant, he sees their easy camaraderie and relaxed body language, the way they joke and call to each other as they work. He is impressed with them—not only because of what he can see on the outside but also for what he senses on the inside.

He is alone, a carpenter who works for his daily bread using his hands. He is beginning a new life of walking the land, spreading the message of a loving God that is carved on his heart. It is what he is called to do; his life's purpose. Though the sea is not his natural environment, he identifies with these men because of their shared experience of manual work and their common faith. He recognizes the value that hardiness, simplicity, and commitment to their jobs holds, because his own father was a carpenter—a working man—and his mother labored over her home and family. He identifies with the commonness of their daily lives because his hometown of Nazareth was just a little plot of land where the pace was determined by the routines of daily life that shaped the hours and gave form to relationships. Yes, he identifies with these fishermen, and as he walks toward them, they look up from their nets and follow his approach. He is a stranger, after all, yet there is something about him that attracts their attention and draws them to him—a connection they feel but cannot explain.

As he nears, he enters into conversation with them, asking about their catch, their families, and their hopes and dreams for the future. At first reluctant to distract themselves from the day's work, they finally respond. There is a quality of attentiveness and respect in this man that compels them to engage him.

They tell him about the local synagogue and how they find comfort and strength in hearing the scriptures explained. They share their hopes that the Messiah will come and drive out the Roman oppressors. They vent their anger over being an occupied people, subject to pagan rulers with their idols and false gods. Being men of action, their words tumble out in a mixture of feelings and awkwardness, but nonetheless, they are honest.

These are neither overly religious men nor pious temple priests. Rather, they are men of spirit and flesh for whom God is real and worship of God is anchored deeply in their hearts. They know about God's faithfulness, and more importantly, they know about God's promises to their ancestors and to them. These are men of faith who believe in one God. They believe that God will send them a savior, a Messiah, who will give them back their homeland. They believe in the Torah with its stories of God's faithfulness from the time of father Abraham. They believe that the Exodus of their ancestors is not just a story from the past but also a promise of the future. These men may not be rabbinical scholars, but they are faith-filled men for whom God is real, present, and active.

We watch as the stranger listens with his whole being and seems to understand their lives, their hearts, their hopes, and their faith. He draws them out and questions which of the teachings of the Torah are most meaningful to them. He seems to have endless time to listen, and they, finding a man who not only knows how to listen but also is able to teach them about the scriptures, are mesmerized. As the conversation continues, these ordinary men are moved in a way they have never known. This man seems to know so much about them and their faith, yet, in his quiet and unassuming way, he says little. They have told him so much about themselves, yet he has shared less. Who is he? Where does he live? Who is his family? When will they see him again?

In this scene, we begin to know not just the disciples but also this Jesus whom we follow. We observe his manner with the fishermen and recognize God's similar way with us. God knows us through and through, and yet God waits for us to share ourselves. We are not forced into relationship; we are invited. In the power of Jesus' listening presence, the fishermen imagined a new life that gave them the courage to leave their nets when they were asked to do so. This is the same listening presence that God offers each of us, through the Holy Spirit, and it has the same power to call forth new life if we allow it.

## Every Invitation Deserves a Response

Returning to the scene, we notice how the squawk of the birds and the chatter of other fishermen remind this small group to focus on their work, to catch enough fish for the day's meal and profit. Talking is fine, but there are tasks to be accomplished and people can't eat if talk is the only food. They make their needs known and prepare their nets for the boats.

The stranger prepares to continue his journey. He has tasted what lies beneath the surface of their features and behaviors. He sees clearly what makes up the basis of their lives: family, the sea, their faith, and their work. He envisions a future that involves them, and he wants them as companions—those who will walk the way with him. Yet all he can do is invite them. They must respond. He is alone now, but he knows that is not what his life is about. If his own calling is to be accomplished, he needs strong, faithful, courageous, creative companions who are passionate in pursuing what they know is right, and more, who love him.

The fishermen want him to stay, to fill them with the food of wisdom and grace, to tell them what the scriptures mean and listen to the joys and sorrows of their hearts. They are torn. They need to accomplish today's work, but they are not willing to let this stranger leave them. They feel trapped by indecision. He ignores their doubt and invites them to leave their nets and walk with him, to give up what they know, the sea, in order to join him as he sets out into the deep of life to fish for those who are hungry for God and spread the good news of God's promise and love.

Matthew's passage doesn't mention their internal conflict, but we can imagine it because we have had others offer us opportunities that seemed so good we wanted to leave everything behind. We know it isn't that easy. We have been conflicted at times, having to choose between two good things, and so we can imagine the inner consternation of the fishermen. "Leave our nets?" they think. "Are you crazy? This is all we know. This is how we live. This is what makes us confident and whole. We are simple men, not learned. We have families. We cannot leave our nets. No way. Never."

But here is Jesus telling them, "If you leave your nets, I will make you fishers of men."

"What?" they think. "What does *that* mean? How do we fish for men?"

Instead of answering all their questions and eliminating all their spoken and unspoken fears, he turns his back and begins to move away. They look into each other's eyes and see there a reflection of what each feels in his own heart. "I do not understand this invitation. What will I tell my family? How will they survive if I'm not here? I don't even know this man—how can I surrender it all and follow him?" Their hearts are on fire, even as their minds reel with unresolved questions. Yet one by one, they drop their nets and walk behind him as he leads the way.

The fishermen-turned-disciples followed their hearts. They listened to the voice within them that said this stranger could be trusted to show them what their hearts yearned to know. Each saw his own deep desires confirmed in the faces of his friends and coworkers. Each gained strength from the truth they experienced in the person of Jesus. Their hearts, their faith, and the confirmation of others gave them the courage to make the changes that would bring their lives to fulfillment and ultimate purpose. They left their nets in exchange for the freedom to follow Jesus.

## What Does the Story Mean Today?

My own first encounter with Christ is seared into my memory, and, as with the fishermen, it changed the path of my life, forever. I was seven, and it was my first Communion. We had been instructed about every motion and response in the ritual, one of which was to return from receiving Communion to kneel with our faces in our hands in order to pray. In those days, I was quite obedient! As I knelt with my face covered, trying to unstick the host from the roof of my mouth, I heard my name, "Linda." It was as clear as a bell, but was no voice I knew. I dared not look up for fear of being reprimanded, so I just knelt there. Again, I heard a voice that seemed external calling, "Linda." I split my fingers apart and stole a peek from side to side, but those around me were face-in-hand. I heard the voice again and it said, "Linda, I want you. Follow me." And it was over. Sister clicked the clicker and we all sat. The Mass ended, the pictures and party followed, and life went on.

What surprises me so many years later is that I was not frightened. It seemed, after the first confusion, to be the most natural thing in the world. I knew immediately, in that inner place where we know the truth, that it was "God." For many people, this might seem a quite significant event, and surely, it was. But it was not jarring or earth-shattering when it happened; the sun did not spin nor did my medal change to gold. I simply heard a voice I did not know but did not fear calling me, claiming me. It took me some years to understand what that experience meant, but throughout the rest of my childhood and teen years it colored my choices and decisions (though not always my behavior). I was not a first-century Palestinian fisherman; yet, I was called to follow Christ. I was given a grace to accept my experience as true and God given, not to deny or dismiss it. Shaping a response that felt authentic and doable was not easy, but there was no doubt in my mind that I must shape one. Every invitation deserves a response.

My experience is unique to me, but the fact of hearing the call to follow Christ and responding to it with our lives is as ancient as Moses and Abraham and as contemporary as a child somewhere in the world at this very moment who realizes God is real and personal. The fishermen found in Jesus the answer to questions they did not even know they had, and they followed him because they could not do otherwise. That's how I felt, and that is what each of us is meant to experience if we allow a personal relationship with Christ to take the primary place in our lives.

Fewer people than ever continue to make their living by fishing, so the meaning of this image of fishermen and Jesus might be lost when we hear it proclaimed in the scriptures. Yet, reflecting on the scripture and seeing it take shape in my own life has taught me that there are at least three truths we can take away from this simple passage that apply to our contemporary lives as followers of Christ:

- Christ identifies with and invites ordinary people to walk with him and carry on his work in this world.

- Christ's invitation is ongoing and comes with a lifetime guarantee of renewal.

- Would-be followers of Christ are engaged with a sense of urgency to assess which "nets" are holding them back from a positive response to Christ's invitation.

Let's examine each of these three truths to see what meaning they may have for our own lives.

### Christ identifies with and invites ordinary people to walk with him and carry on his work in this world

This first truth brings the joy and, perhaps for some, astonishment in realizing that each of us qualifies to be one of Christ's friends and disciples. Because we exist, we are eligible. We are "good enough" just as we are to be chosen by Jesus Christ to walk with him and to help him to accomplish his purpose. We don't have to be famous, rich, educated, influential, or blessed with special talents in order to become a member of Christ's inner circle of companions; all are welcome and all are called. We simply have to "show up," to be aware and alert to Christ's presence asking us to follow. If a seven-year-old, born of first-generation immigrants, without any special skills or orientation, as I was when I heard my call, can be offered an invitation to follow Christ, then all are worthy. It isn't about earning our call, it's about recognizing it. We tend to think that the apostles were the only ones Christ called. They weren't. In addition to the named and unnamed men and women of the gospels, there are all those who were called but who were too afraid to follow, and thus, we never learn of them.

We can recognize Christ's call at any age, in any circumstance. Children are so close to the sacred and their imaginations are so alive that they are able to connect with the mystical more quickly and surely than adult cynicism sometimes will allow. To plant the seeds of knowing Christ by reading Bible stories and imagining the details, as we did in this story of the fishermen, offers children a path for exploring the voice of

16

STEP ONE

God in their own lives. My childhood faith was nurtured in a Catholic school where incorporating God into my daily life became second nature. But the important thing is to develop our religious imagination from our earliest years, so when a significant spiritual experience occurs, we are ready to receive it. Like the fishermen, my faith and my environment formed my consciousness of God's abiding presence. We can and must create this kind of environment for others.

Our call may come at work where our coworkers seek not only a paycheck but also meaning for the daily struggle. Our good works and genuine desire to cooperate, collaborate, and support others provide endless opportunities both to witness to God's faithfulness and power in our lives and to hear God's call through the witness of others. To see work as an opportunity to cooperate with God in the ongoing creation of the world is a powerful tool for evangelization and a profound way to realize that God is calling us to serve through our work. To place people before things, profit, or personal gain is to model our lives on the person of Jesus, who laid down his life for his friends. The fishermen were not just working because they had to; they valued their work. It gave their lives meaning, and their scriptures honored work as part of God's plan. God used their work environment as the vehicle for Christ to enter and change their lives. God wants to use our work environments in the same way.

Most poignantly perhaps, we meet Christ in the faces around our dining tables—those that seek the food of unconditional love and share our daily dance, our concerns, our fears, and our joys and sorrows. There are no relationships more intimate, soul forming or difficult than those forged in family life. Here the call to discipleship looks like diaper changing or offering a listening ear when we're tired and stressed. We don't meet Christ by running from the routines of our lives—nor by overlooking the presence of God in those with whom we share family life—but by enmeshing ourselves in those routines and those people and doing what belongs to us to do with a heart of right intention and effort. It is this very "everydayness" of life that embodies our call to join Christ and take part in his work in the world; it is in the sea of our daily lives where the "fish" that Christ seeks can be found. It is here that we cast our nets as his disciples.

### Christ's invitation is ongoing and comes with a lifetime guarantee of renewal

Christ calls us to change our lives and become disciples on a daily basis—sometimes, moment to moment. Christ called those he chose, and they were limited not by his call but by their courage to respond. If we can't quite manage to surrender our old used nets today—if our hearts are too hard or filled up to hear his voice right now or we just can't seem to see "how" we will do what our hearts inspire—we must hang on, because perhaps tomorrow, or the next day, or next year we will be ready. Perhaps then we will find the courage and the passion to surrender our nets, that is, what is familiar, comfortable, and safe, in order to change and to follow. The reality is that conversion, that change of heart that refocuses us on Christ and his purpose, is an ongoing process, not a one-time thing.

Conversion is a response to state of heart that provides a receptive openness to the presence of Christ and the action of the Holy Spirit. It isn't just about the mountaintop; it isn't about emotion. Conversion happens in a moment of clarity that demands an inner change. It's a moment of truth that reveals your soul and your life's purpose. The voice I heard was not just a call to serve Christ, it was a moment of conversion in my young soul. It was a turning toward Christ. Daily, repeatedly,

God offers unending invitations to drop everything that we've
been trained to think is important and that others tell us is
important, and instead, to turn toward Christ, to follow the
only One who truly is important and whose relationship is
something we want and need more than all else. It's a paradoxical yet comforting thought, this ongoing invitation to conversion. It creates a pocket of hope that gives us the courage
to move forward.

### Would-be followers of Christ have to assess when to cast a net and when to let it go

The final of our threefold truth from this story is the one that
blindsides us. What will it mean to embrace this quiet, articu-
late, insightful stranger wholeheartedly, with all we are and all
we possess? Like the fishermen, we wonder how we can possibly put down our nets and follow. We think, "I don't even own
a net, so what is it that Christ is asking of me in this scripture?"

Here's the truth. The nets are a metaphor for what we are
using to fill up our lives right now. The nets are what we have
labeled "essential" for our well-being. The nets are those we
think cannot survive without us, or what we cannot live without. The nets are those whom we use as an excuse for not being
about the mission of Christ in this world—spouse or kids, parents or friends, and jobs. The nets are those things that hold
the center place in our hearts, where Christ is trying to take
up residence; they are the habits we've acquired whether or
not they are helpful and healthy. The nets are not necessarily
bad, rather, they are obstacles to following Christ when we use
them as excuses for not changing.

The nets provide an image for our call to conversion, and
it is in discerning what to keep and what to give up that we
experience the sting of following Christ. It isn't easy to walk in

Christ's footsteps because we know the end of the story that the
fishermen did not know on that day they decided to leave the
sea. We know, with the hindsight of over two thousand years,
that walking with Jesus, as the disciples did, leads to Jerusalem
and death. Sorting the nets and sacrificing some things so that
only those parts of us that respond to the call of Christ are left is
the first step in this disciple's walk to Jerusalem. It is a sample
of the small deaths that words like discipleship and conversion
imply. The good news is that we also know that in this story
ending, new life comes after death.

## Conversion Stings

The sting of this first step of discipleship, **surrendering our
nets**, is that from the beginning a disciple is asked to sacrifice
in order to follow Christ. Make no mistake about it, it is a
choice—a daily choice. Like the fishermen, when Christ asks
us to leave our nets, he is asking us to reevaluate our lives, our
relationships, and our goals and mission, all the good people
and things with which we surround ourselves and have spent
so much time, energy, and treasure accumulating. The sting
is in realizing that, while good, if we make any of these an
excuse for not changing and embracing the priorities Christ
has given us, we won't be able to be his faithful companion—
not because we are not worthy and not because Christ does
not want us, but because that place of companionship and
discipleship is reserved for those willing to place Christ and
his mission before all others.

Perhaps this sounds too overwhelming or simply impos-
sible to do. If so, imagine this conversation: "But what about
those I love, who depend on me?" And Christ says, "Can you
embrace them with my love, without suffocating them or using
them as a crutch to avoid what I want you to do?" "What about
my livelihood?" we worry. He answers, "Can you work so that

the glory goes to God and use each opportunity of interaction as a way to proclaim my love?" "What about my treasures?" we sigh. And Christ gently whispers, "Can you live simply so that others have access to resources? Can you give from your need to those whose need is greater? Can you depend on me to provide?" It's about trusting that the turn toward Christ will give you what you need to take the next step.

When I heard Christ's call as a girl of seven, I did not have answers to these questions. I didn't even know these questions existed. What I did know at the core of my being was that God loved me and wanted my love in return. What it would take to give that love seemed easy at the time. It has taken me a lifetime of conversion, and many stings along the way, to better understand what real love is, what real following entails. And it all starts with surrendering our nets.

## ☀ Questions
### for Reflection, Journaling, and Discussion

1.  Imagine yourself as one of the fishermen working with your nets at the sea's shore when a stranger's approach attracts your attention. What do you feel? What do you do?

2.  Describe a time when you heard Christ's call to follow him. What change was involved? Did it sting? What did you do?

3.  Name the "nets" in your life that have "top priority" status for you. Which nets do you need to surrender or reprioritize in order to follow Christ more closely? How do these choices make you feel? What will you do?

4.  Who are those into whose eyes you can look for affirmation of your call to follow Christ more closely? When and how will you discuss this invitation with them?

5. Describe your understanding of discipleship and Christ's conversation with you. How are you presently following him? What nudges do you receive that point out there is more being asked?

## ☀ Journal Your Thoughts: Let Go

## A Ritual for Surrendering Your Nets

- Using your reflection and journaling from the section above as a source of truth and wisdom, find or make a symbol of each net you must mend or surrender in order to follow Christ as his disciple. For example, if you fear how your family might react to your choice to be a more active follower of Christ, find a family picture to use as a symbol. If you lack the courage to witness to Christ at your workplace, choose a symbol of your work.

- Once you have a symbol *for each net* that stands between you and deeper discipleship, do the following:

* Place your symbols on your prayer table along with a candle, a metal or ceramic plate, and a small cloth/napkin.
* Each day, as part of your prayer, light the candle, hold one of the symbols, and pray the prayer below.
* As you reach a point (eventually) when you are ready to surrender that particular net that holds you back from embracing Christ fully, burn or cover that symbol. Continue this ritual until all are "left behind." If you realize other nets you didn't originally identify, simply continue the practice.

Finally, as we prepare for step two of *Walking the Disciple's Path*, keep in mind that conversion is a lifelong journey. There is no one right way to experience Christ's presence in our lives, nor is there any one way to experience Christ's call. Everyone baptized in Christ is offered an ongoing invitation to deepen the relationship. Each day is a new day to begin or to continue the process. We do not walk this path alone. In addition to all those other followers, we have Christ himself, who walks alongside and whose Spirit leads the way.

## ☀ A Prayer
### for Letting Go

Jesus, you spent your life calling those who hunger for God to follow you, for you are the Way.

You showed that God is very near, but only those with eyes to see, hearts to respond, and courage to change will find God.

Embrace me this day, O Lord. Fill me with your love and the courage to leave those nets that no longer help me to do your will, to follow you, to trust in your care and faithfulness, and to respond to your call to go where you lead. Amen.

# Live as a Blessing

When Jesus saw the crowds, he went up the mountain; and after he sat down, his disciples came to him. Then he began to speak, and taught them, saying: "Blessed are the poor in spirit, for theirs is the kingdom of heaven. Blessed are those who mourn for they will be comforted. Blessed are the meek, for they will inherit the earth. Blessed are those who hunger and thirst for righteousness, for they will be filled. Blessed are the merciful, for they will receive mercy. Blessed are the pure in heart, for they will see God. Blessed are the peacemakers for they will be called children of God. Blessed are those who are persecuted for righteousness sake, for theirs is the kingdom of heaven. Blessed are you when people revile you and persecute you and utter all kinds of evil against you falsely on my account. Rejoice and be glad for your reward is great in heaven, for in the same way they persecuted the prophets who were before you."

Matthew 5:1–12

## Imagine and Reflect

The crowds have grown in recent days.

Their cries for healing rise like dust in the desert.

The Teacher is weary and in need of solitude

As he moves to the mountainside and waits for his disciples
   to follow.

Ready to teach them the most important lessons of their lives,

His voice is confident as he describes the kingdom of heaven.

His face is serene as each word carves a place within them,

Turning their world upside-down.

He trusts them to change their hearts;

To absorb the values that he offers.

He invites them to live as a blessing for others

All the days of their lives.

Here is the Rabbi, forming his disciples;

The Teacher, educating his students.

Here is Jesus, painting a picture of what a blessed life looks
   like.

They have yet to learn how painful it is to be so blessed.

## Taking the Second Step

In Matthew's gospel, we are introduced to Jesus in his teaching ministry. He teaches those who will, in turn, teach others. This is what rabbis do—form a community of disciples who will spread their Rabbi's interpretation of the Torah. So, in this scene, we have Jesus offering his disciples the core values of his teaching and the secret to what will make life worth living. Accepting and living these teachings forms the second step of the disciple's path: to embody these blessings as we follow Christ. It is the source of what will become both the fishermen-disciples' and our joy.

## Entering the Scripture Story:
## Jesus the Rabbi-Teacher

In this gospel scene, we are told that Jesus and his disciples go to a mountain, which for the Jews was a traditional place of encounter with God. We stand back a bit and watch as Jesus gives his followers a "study guide" in the form of eight characteristics of those who would follow him. We hear him emphasize that those who develop these characteristics will live blessed lives. It is comforting to realize that we, too, are being given a blueprint upon which we can build a happy life. And then, like the early disciples, we realize that we do not yet understand what "happy" means.

The "blessed attitudes" begin chapter 5 of Matthew's gospel, and he closes it on yet another mountain, where the risen Christ sends his now battle-tested disciples out to make new disciples. The pattern of teacher-student, transmitter of wisdom–wisdom seeker, is a classic rabbinical method of passing on truth to a bevy of disciples. The formation that Jesus gives consists in two types of teaching: word of mouth, that is, orally passing on knowledge and wisdom; and behavior modeling, or demonstrating what such teaching looks like when lived. In both forms we experience Matthew's Jesus as mentor and teacher.

This mountain classroom provides the disciples with an environment where they can rest in his presence, away from the growing crowds. Here he can speak to them directly, in an unhurried way. Scholars believe that the "sermon" Jesus gave on that mountain was too lengthy to have been delivered at one sitting and is probably a collection of many of Jesus' teachings, pulled together in a tidy bundle not unlike a speech that describes a person's vision of life. The Sermon on the Mount, as we know it, and from which this chapter draws its focus, is Jesus' vision of life under God's rule. He teaches that the kingdom of heaven is all around us, within us. It is accessible, existing wherever God is uppermost, whenever anyone chooses to make God the ruler of life and to serve God first. He promotes the understanding that happiness is not based on superficial things but on a way of life that is marked by union with God and kingdom values.

This is the way all successful movements begin. The founder has a vision of life and describes a way to live it. That vision is shared with others. Those who believe in the vision embrace and follow it. If the vision has depth, and gives life, then the followers are inspired to spread the vision and the group expands again. New "disciples" are called and formed. This is what we see Jesus doing in this scripture, sharing his vision in order to form his followers who will replicate the process.

We, his contemporary followers, are asked to understand that vision as well. For in responding to Christ's call we are asked to imagine another definition of happiness, to live as a blessing for ourselves and others. Once again, Jesus forms our religious imagination and paints a picture of a deep and satisfying life that can be ours if we accept his teaching and live it. Notice that Jesus begins by describing the first blessing that should define our lives: the blessing of being poor in spirit. He tells us that we can be happy if we become poor in spirit.

### The poor in spirit

The fishermen, now known as disciples and followers of Jesus of Nazareth, have surrendered their nets and refocused their lives on walking with Jesus. This new life is exhilarating, but it also involves long, hot days in the Judean sun and cool, uncomfortable nights sleeping wherever a place can be found, often out of doors and open to the elements. As this passage implies, as Jesus' message and word of his healing power spread from town to town, the crowds grow larger and more demanding. The fact that he heals people intensifies the clamor for his attention. The disciples have their hands full trying to protect Jesus from the crowds that press around him, while also organizing his encounters with the sick and providing for their small community's daily needs.

On this day, it seems everyone is tired, as is implied when Matthew tells us that "Jesus saw the crowd," and it seems that Jesus is in need of solitude as well as an opportunity to clarify his thoughts and vision for his disciples. Jesus understands that his followers need formation in the vision that animates all that he says and does, for what he chooses to do and those whom he serves do not fit past patterns, nor do the norms that have guided past prophetic leaders guide him. So often the disciples seem not to understand Jesus' choices. Now he will explain. It is here that we begin to imagine the story.

Picture the scene. It has been a long day, filled with healing. Jesus is tired and indicates a need for rest by walking up a mountain path and finding a shady place to sit, away from the crowd. The disciples follow him, and in the intimacy of their small group he begins to share with them: "Blessed are the poor in spirit."

Undoubtedly, the disciples are not expecting this conversation and may be puzzled. They may think, "Perhaps we misunderstood him? What could he possibly mean?" Jesus goes on, "The poor will inherit the kingdom . . ." But they think, "This doesn't make sense. The poor we know beg in the streets. They are ignored if they are lucky; otherwise, they are harassed, abused, and left to die." In their experience, as in ours, the poor inherit nothing but misery. For this group of former fishermen, tax collectors, and itinerant laborers, such an image as "poor in spirit" is beyond their imaginations and perhaps they hear only the word "poor." They lived in a society in which the poor and powerless were invisible, to a large extent, avoided and treated as "unclean." Now, the Teacher says that the poor will be given the kingdom of heaven. He even uses the word *makaroi*, translated into Greek as "blessed," to describe them. Some translations also use the Hebrew word *ashrei*, or happy. How can being poor lead to happiness? How is it a blessing? Or is this a different poverty of which he speaks and a different understanding of happiness?

The Beatitudes are Jesus' vision statement. Through them, he describes which principles and values form the foundation of a world where God reigns. He shows that in God's kingdom there is a different pecking order than the one to which we have become accustomed. In God's kingdom, happiness and experiencing life as a blessing are found in what comes from the inside; it is first and foremost measured in the focus and quality of one's spirit, not one's bank account or outward success. Kingdom success is about being "poor in spirit." Blessing, that state of being dependent on God's grace, is something we can all attain, if we choose.

It is no mistake that Jesus places this "poor in spirit" blessing first. Like the first of the commandments given to Moses on another mountain, it is the foundation on which the rest are built. "Blessed are the poor in spirit." It is a call to conversion, and once again the disciples feel the sting. Their Master seems to say that in order to live all the values that follow this one, in order to experience a life of blessing and inner happiness, a disciple is to learn from the poor in spirit, to sit at the feet of the "little ones," and to soak in their gift to us. But what is that gift on which we will base our own blessed lives?

Essentially, the poor in spirit offer us a glimpse of the kind of faith and trust that depends on God alone. It is this we will need to cultivate in order to embrace the essential attitudes of the kingdom. We see glimpses of the poor in spirit in many gospel stories. Remember the healing of the leper? What kind of trust does it take for a leper to break through a crowd and centuries of cultural taboos to ask for healing? Or, think about the story of the Samaritan woman? What type of trust is needed for a Samaritan woman to give water to a Jewish man? As Matthew tells it, being poor in spirit isn't simply about material wealth or poverty—they are not the most important things at stake. Being poor in spirit is about changing our hearts, breaking them open so that what is within can spill out and what is needed can fill us up. It is about seeing rightly that God is in charge of our lives and, with God, all things are possible. This is the insight that brings about happiness and wakes us up to blessing.

### One sees rightly with the heart

The poor in spirit teach us by exposing the truth of their hearts. Cultivating a relationship with God is about three things: behaviors, motives, and values. Throughout the scriptures we hear that it isn't enough to "do" something; the doing needs to come from the right motivation, and our reasons need to be based on kingdom values. The scriptures are filled with those who say they love God but then do repulsive or harmful things to themselves or others. Intuitively, we understand that inconsistency between what we say we believe and what we then do is not of God. One of the qualities that attract us to Jesus is his genuine consistency of motive and behavior. He does all for the love of God, to bring about God's kingdom—God's reign. As we read in 1 Samuel 16:7, "Man looks at the outward appearances, but the Lord looks at the heart." Jesus' heart is in full union with God.

Our Jewish ancestors in faith understood this truth: All of life emanates from the heart. Christian heroes over the centuries knew it as well: It is with the heart that one sees rightly. Anyone who lives united to God knows this to be true: Life revolves around the heart not just physically but also spiritually.

The word *heart* is found more than 630 times in the scriptures, and the Jewish worldview taught that the heart was the life force and organizing principle of the entire body, mind, and spirit. Jesus demonstrated both the blessings and the consequences of living from the heart, and the scriptures provide a stethoscope for evaluating the health of our own hearts. "For the word of God is living and active. Sharper than any double-edged sword, it penetrates even to dividing soul and spirit, joints and marrow; it judges the thoughts and attitudes of the heart" (Heb. 4:12).

What God desires from us, followers and disciples of Jesus, is not outward conformity but inner surrender—a surrender of the heart. Wherever we look in the scripture, Jesus condemned those whose lips held praise of God but whose hearts were closed to others. The poor in spirit understand that the life of the heart is lived by choice, not the whims of emotion. The poor in spirit choose not to guard their hearts from the presence of God, nor protect them from God's in-breaking. Their lives lie open to the Gospel's song—vulnerable and dependent on God's care and mercy. In order to live this dependency, they choose to surrender themselves to God's providence, to take nothing for granted, to see themselves in a true light—needy of God's mercy for survival—and to empty themselves so that God can pitch his tent within them.

When we are poor in spirit, we approach God on our knees, for we see ourselves honestly. We examine not only our consciences but also our motives, values, and the ways in which we live these out. The poor in spirit understand there can be no dichotomy between what we say and do and what we believe and value. If the only questions are "What do I believe?" or "How well do I understand?" then we, disciples, will never engage in conversion and following Christ will forever remain an intellectual discussion, not a world-transforming event.

The faithful disciple asks instead, "How true is my heart?" "What is it that my heart desires?" "What brings inner happiness to my heart?" The test of our ongoing conversion and conformity to the heart of Christ is not simply what we are doing but also what is taking place in our hearts as we act and how well the two are integrated. To probe the health of our hearts is to probe our motives, attitudes, and character—all of which lead to behaviors and choices. Jesus was trying to teach us that the poor in spirit cultivate attitudes that bear fruit as we acknowledge God's blessing and care.

## Cultivate Humility, Vulnerability, and Trust in God

To be poor in spirit is to be humble, to live as though all depended on God, to know your place in the universe, to admit you are not in control, and to trust the One who is.

To be poor in spirit is to understand emptiness and vulnerability not as it's written in a book but as it's lived in the deep recesses of a broken heart.

To be poor in spirit is to trust that God will provide, to claim no strength as your own, to believe that no weakness is irreversible, and to bless the mighty One who does great things.

The fishermen-disciples did not run away from their Teacher's difficult lesson on that mountain because, even while it startled them, it also inspired them. They reflected on its meaning; they examined their hearts as they continued to walk with Jesus; and they watched as he showed them what "poor in spirit" looked like in the flesh—even to emptying himself on the Cross, totally dependent on his Abba's love and mercy. They realized, as we are striving to do, that this lesson in reframing our understanding of blessing and happiness is the secret to a deeply fulfilling life.

Three qualities distinguish the poor in spirit and each is a quality we need to cultivate as we walk this second step on the disciple's path.

### Humility

For many, humility means debasing oneself or selling oneself short, denying our gifts and talents. Rather, true humility is realizing that all we have has been given to us by a gracious and generous God. This realization is what gives perseverance to the poor in spirit in the face of difficulty and hardship. It's an understanding that moderates inordinate pride, which sometimes can show itself as arrogant or "self-made" overconfidence, neither of which is becoming to a follower of Christ. Humility helps the poor in spirit to know our place in the universe and relinquish the role only God can hold.

### Vulnerability

Vulnerability is the ability to allow our deepest emotions to be at the service of others, to "reveal our own wounds" in the attempt to heal another. It is a scary quality to cultivate in a society that proclaims strength at all cost, that exploits violence and ridicules any "soft" emotion like tenderness, compromise, forgiveness, or compassion. The poor in spirit understand vulnerability, for their survival is often dependent on the kindness of others who are willing and able to empathize with them. They wear their true lives for all to see; they hide nothing of who they are. They recognize that vulnerability is what creates a compassionate heart, for it is the outward sign of inward empathy, a heart most like their Teacher and Lord.

### Trust

Trust is the life song of the poor in spirit. To trust in God is to know that the present picture is not the whole story. To trust in God is to believe that the story of our lives is being written not by our works alone but by God who is working in and through the circumstances of our lives, even when we cannot understand what is happening. To trust in God is to believe that we are not the final arbiters of our lives but that, whatever the future holds, God holds the future. When we are poor in spirit, we trust in God and let go of both control and fear. We cannot cease to do our part in creating a future that is livable and blessed. But we do not need to accept the burden of thinking that it all rests on our shoulders.

## What Does the Story Mean Today?

I was born into a middle-class family, of parents whose parents were immigrants and who themselves were self-employed. My parents worked hard building a good life for us. Their hours were long, and we seldom had weekday meals together because one parent was always "in the store." Since my maternal grandfather lived with us, we were a multigenerational family, and my brother and I had the blessing of several mentors, "parents," and role models.

My dad and my grandfather couldn't have been more different in temperament, abilities, and attitudes toward life. They were both wonderful men, each in his singular way, and I loved them both mightily. Yet even as a small girl I felt an inner conflict trying to discern how I could love two such different men. Whose "way" was right? Whose advice was the wisest?

Whose vision of life would I adopt as my vision? Today, I realize that they both influenced my forming womanhood. But in the early years, awakening to the need to choose a vision of life that would guide my own life was not so easily tackled.

My dad was a high-energy, opinionated, politically connected, hard-driving man. He had a limited education because, as the eldest in his immigrant family, he was pulled out of school to get a job. He regretted that lost education all of his life, yet he didn't hesitate to do what was needed for his family and to contribute to the education of his younger siblings. After serving honorably in the Second World War, Dad married my mother and started his own business. He wanted to be involved and did so within the professional organizations geared to his business and in politics. In both, he was a leader who was fearless in speaking up for the "little guys." Dad loved sports, Italian singers and musicians, family gatherings, and his own family—not necessarily in that order. He had little time for outside activities and had to close the store in order to come to our school events, which he never missed.

For all his good qualities, Dad also had a ferocious temper and a threatening and demeaning way of expressing it. He wasn't overtly religious though he came from a religious family. Going to church wasn't high on his list, and I believe it had somewhat to do with working so late on Saturday night with only Sunday as a day of "rest." But every big religious occasion saw my dad present. The vision of life Dad handed on to us was to go to school, get a great job, become wealthy, and vote Republican. A close, personal relationship with Jesus wasn't high on the articulated list, and even when he died I don't think he fully understood how or why that was so important to my life. Though I believe he realized how it had directed my life.

My maternal grandfather, on the other hand, was himself an immigrant, coming to this country as a fourteen-year-old orphan. For all of my life, I either lived upstairs from my maternal grandparents or my grandfather lived in our home. He was always employed on the railroad. My grandmother died at fifty-three, and my aunt, my mother's only sister, was left mentally impaired by a bout of measles and died young. Grampa was no stranger to hard times or sorrow.

Grampa was a gentle, caring presence in our lives. He was our favorite babysitter, cutting apples and telling stories. His room held a statue of the Sacred Heart with a votive candle that I now have in my home. While not overtly religious, his faith seemed to permeate him. He had a great singing voice, was a talented chef, and was quite able to take care of a home. Grampa also was a good listener who always had time to hear my fears and teach me yet one more thing. His vision of life was to live quietly, to be kind to others, to do what was needed for our family, and to be unobtrusive but supportive. He and Dad clashed at times, and it was in their conflict that I found the grist to decide what I valued. My Grampa was a wonderful role model for how the poor in spirit approach life. He exhibited the humility, vulnerability, and trust in God that I later learned were qualities of the poor in spirit and of the life of discipleship.

All of us have role models through whose lives we explore and understand the teaching of Christ. For me it was my grandfather. Acknowledging this doesn't diminish my dad's many great qualities, and the contrast between the two men allowed me to test my own appreciation for the value and importance of poverty of spirit long before I understood the term. Many would-be twenty-first-century disciples react with shock, dismay, or confusion when confronted with Christ's teachings in the Beatitudes, especially the teaching regarding the poor in spirit. Some even harden their hearts and close their ears when they meet that teaching. For to be poor in spirit implies the ultimate Gospel paradox: When I am weak, then I am strong. That hardly sounds like a recipe for happiness, but that's what makes it countercultural. Living Gospel attitudes leads to an inner purification that opens room for God to have a home, and when God is in residence, we experience the reward of bless-edness, of inner joy, regardless of the outward circumstances.

As in step one (surrendering our nets), the scripture of this second step (live as a blessing) has three lessons to help us move forward on the disciple's path:

- Depend on God's mercy.
- Choose your role models carefully.
- Live simply.

### Depend on God's mercy

Surely this is a lesson the poor in spirit know all too well—we can depend on nothing but God. There is no rank or status, education, wealth, privilege, social standing, or talent more powerful than the Creator of life. There are no disciples, believ-ers, followers, devotees, or students who can survive on their own wits, without God's intervention.

Humility comes from acknowledging our limitations, accepting our place and purpose in God's plan, and realizing our talents did not create the universe. Rather, the poor in spirit live in a state of exposure, relying on God to be our shield. We place ourselves on the line, believing that God will keep us safe. We open ourselves to the direction God leads and are sensitive to the voice of God guiding our thoughts and actions.

### Carefully choose your role models

The poor in spirit are not impressed by material possessions, for we know these are subject to breakage and deterioration.

While we like nice things, we are not awed by fancy clothes or homes because we know that these do not determine the quality of our inner happiness or of our relationship with God and others. We are drawn not to persuasive words or wise observations but to the excellence of compassion, service, and genuine community the speaker demonstrates every day, for we know that talk doesn't cost anything, while action does. The poor in spirit seek to imitate Jesus, for we see in him one who understands and walks God's way.

### Live simply

Finally, the poor in spirit teach us that we don't need all that we have or want. Living simply provides inner calm and space in which to reflect on God's word and will. Having just what is needed uses less time and money to clean and secure, salvaging more time and resource for service; it provides a common link of compassion to those who have little and suffer; and it measures our creativity. Living simply allows our lives, minds, and hearts to go uncluttered, receptive to God's word and action. It also inspires us to trust in God's providence, rather than money and material possessions. God provides what is needed.

 ## Questions

## for Reflection, Journaling, and Discussion

1.  What reactions do the words *vulnerability*, *humility*, and *trust* evoke in you? With whom are you most able to be vulnerable? What does it take for you to trust another? Are you able to be vulnerable and trusting with God?

2.  On a scale of one to ten (with ten being very important), how would you evaluate your need for or attachment to

your possessions? Is there a relationship between what you have and the degree to which you trust in God?

3.  To be poor in spirit is at the heart of being able to live the Beatitudes in spirit as well as in fact. After reading about step two on the disciple's path, how would you describe your own poverty of spirit? Who models this spirit best for you at this time? What can you do to learn from this person, and what steps will you take to put that learning into action?

4.  The kingdom of God is the flip side of the everyday life we encounter in the twenty-first-century world around us. Which part of your environment offers you an invitation to better witness to the kingdom values Jesus gave the disciples? When and how can you give better witness?

## ☀ Journal Your Thoughts:
### Gratitude and Forgiveness

## A Ritual for Growing in Humility

Each evening, before sleep, settle yourself in bed and do the following:

- Close your eyes and recall the events throughout the day.

- Allow the faces of people you encountered today to run before the dark spaces behind your eyes.

- Remember the conversations you had and the thoughts and feelings that pressed on you.

- Give thanks to God for each time you were able to interact in a way that imitates Christ.

- Ask for forgiveness for each time you failed to be poor in spirit, that is, humble and open, receptive and vulnerable, and dependent on and trusting in God.

Close with the prayer below.

 A Prayer

## for the Poor in Spirit

Jesus, teach me to be poor in spirit. Instruct me in the ways of humility. Set my heart on the right path, open and vulnerable, committed to you above all else. Give me the grace to learn from you who are meek and humble of heart and to recognize in your grace-filled life the model for my own. Amen.

## STEP THREE

# Love
# Your
# Enemies

Y ou have heard that it was said, "You shall love
your neighbor and hate your enemy." But I say
to you, "love your enemies and pray for those
who persecute you so that you may be children of your
Father in heaven; for he makes his sun to rise on the evil
and on the good, and sends rain on the righteous and
on the unrighteous. For if you love those who love you,
what reward do you have? . . . Be perfect, therefore, as
your heavenly Father is perfect."

Matthew 5:43–46, 48

## Imagine and Reflect

Turning the other cheek is easy
Until the pain comes,
Until your vulnerability is seen as submission rather than the
     power of choice,
Until the violence in another's heart is so beyond control
Your gesture of peace
Provokes the desire to hurt . . . to conquer.
Loving your enemy is as easy as
Turning the other cheek,
And we all know how hard that is.

## Love

Our third step concentrates on our understanding of love, the core of Jesus' teaching, God's self-definition (1 Jn 4:8), and the essence of what it means to be a Christian.

As we turn our thoughts to Gospel love, it might be good to recall our first two steps on the disciple's path. In surrendering our nets, we learned that we have to let go of whatever has become an obstacle to following Christ, if we want to hear his call. Our second step taught us to redefine blessing as the inner happiness that comes from trusting and depending on God. This third step follows naturally, pointing out that, once we have committed to follow Christ and to trust that God will lead and provide for us, we are ready to love ourselves, God, and others more fully. The love described in this step seems easily within our grasp until Jesus starts to elaborate on the meaning of *neighbor*, which he tells us includes "enemies."

## *Entering the Scripture Story:*
## *Love Is a Choice*

Loving my enemies has been one of the hardest steps to take along my own spiritual walk with Christ. Yes, it's inspiring and gives me something to strive for, but the reality is that when I experience an "enemy," the last thing I'm inclined to do is to love. In Matthew's gospel, Jesus' thoughts on loving enemies are one of several teachings that follow and give flesh to the Beatitudes. It is a way of giving life to that elusive inner happiness that we explored in step two. This third step takes things to a very personal place because it goes against everything we've ever learned, culturally, about how to treat an enemy.

When those boys were pelting me with small stones because I was different, was I supposed to love them? What would that love look like? Is it even possible? Apparently Jesus believed that love in the face of hostility is possible. He showed us how to do it in his own life. He revealed to us— when he held back Peter's sword, when he fed Judas his body and blood, when he didn't condemn Pilate, and at so many other times—this is how God shows that God is love. Jesus was alluding to the psalms when he reminded us that God's love encompasses both evildoers and the good; that God loves inclusively, offering to all the same passionate and compassionate heart; that God's love does not condemn but allows for our freedom to choose; and that God does not use his anger for vengeance or violence but for healing and setting things right. Jesus was not condemning the Torah's version of love "for those we know"; rather, he was expanding and fulfilling it.

Our reflection in this chapter invites us to understand that living Gospel love brings its own reward of inner peace, authentic relationships, and union with God.

The Greek verb used for love in this scripture passage is *agapao*, which means to love unconditionally and sacrificially, as God loves us and as God loved Jesus. Jesus chooses to use this verb that describes the highest, purest, and most noble form of love. It is a kind of love that is not motivated by self-interest, as much love is, but is the kind of love God offers us. *Agapao* is not a feeling but a choice to live and act in such a way as to reveal that God lives not only in us but in all others as well. Gospel love as revealed by Jesus and addressed in this passage indicates that, unlike the Old Testament view that the neighbor they were to love was another Israelite and not a stranger, Gospel love sees the neighbor as everyone—there are no strangers. This contrast is at the heart of Jesus' teaching on love and our path of discipleship.

Gospel love is a daily choice to meet the difficulties and the joys of relationship—personal, national, or international—with peace, fidelity, and harmony. When we do, we experience blessing for ourselves and others.

Gospel love holds up the value of "forever" and the model of a God whose love is unconditional and everlasting, even when circumstances are painful. When we live in that same way, we reap the strength and fidelity we seek.

Gospel love, unlike romantic love, isn't about what the lover feels but about what the loved one needs. And as we live life through the eyes of "the other," we come closest to the kind of love Jesus lived and to the path we are asked to walk.

Gospel love is tough stuff. It isn't hyperbole; it's active, not passive. It knows how to endure. It resides in the will as well as in the heart. We show Gospel love when we treat harshness with kindness, when we help people with whom we have nothing in common, and when we are willing to sacrifice our own comfort, opinion, or possessions in order to foster relationships of equality, care, and harmony.

Gospel love is a companion to our other discipleship choices, clearing away the obstacles to hearing Christ's call and trusting in God's care. As we cultivate this love that is God's own way of being, we'll be guided by three things:

- the teachings of Jesus,
- the good of the beloved,
- and the image of the Cross.

### The teachings of Jesus

The teachings of Jesus are the heart of the Gospel, and in each and every case, they point to the meaning of love and how to make it real in everyday life. When we look at Jesus, we believe that he is the embodiment of who God is, and we learn in 1 John 4:16 that "God is love." We also know that Jesus formed his own understanding of what it means to be a human being made in the image and likeness of a God who is love. And that's what each of us needs to do, to understand that at our core we are love and we are made by and for love.

The love Jesus embodied as a human person, which is the basis for our own Christian love, takes the love eye off of the self and focuses it on "the other." Jesus' love stretched beyond himself: It was big enough, deep enough, and true enough to include all others, regardless of their statuses or their responses. He generously gave this love to the sick, the dying, unbelieving Roman soldiers, his captors, women, Samaritans, high priests, Pharisees and scribes who collaborated to kill him, and to anyone who came forward to receive it. This is the love we are meant to offer others. It is what we strive to incorporate into our own way of loving, as difficult as that may be at times.

In every teaching of Jesus, even when the word *love* is not mentioned, the goal is to teach the meaning of love—that love that God has for us, that we are to have for ourselves and others, that is unconditional and unending, and that led Jesus to a cross between two thieves on a Jerusalem hilltop. It's the kind of love that keeps wives and husbands at their spouse's hospital bed for days, months, or even years, in faithful witness and support. It's the kind of love that causes us to carry signs in support of justice or to offer a kidney to a stranger who will die without it. The teaching of Jesus on *agapao* is at work within us when we love in that way. The blessings of joy and equanimity we receive confirm for us that we are on the right path.

### The good of the beloved

The good of the beloved is the overriding motivation of Jesus' acceptance of his suffering and death. It was for love of us that Jesus came into the world and for love of us that he died. Every Christian professes this creed, yet we tend to forget its powerful meaning. Gospel love is meant not to be exclusive, "Jesus and me," but to explode outward and benefit others. The Gospel love that Jesus lived shows us how to be a person who lives for the common good. For a follower of Christ, discipleship takes the form of the cross—arms raised upward to God in love and praise and outward to others in service and sacrifice. We practice this kind of love every time we serve another's needs, sacrifice our personal choice or opinion so that another can be affirmed, or rejoice in the good that others do rather than point out their failings. When we live our love for the common good, we are blessed with community, with the joy of seeing good achieved, and with a sense of the bigger purpose of our lives.

### The image of the Cross

The image of the Cross is a fearsome image for some, but for those who walk with Christ, it evokes gratitude for a love that is so great someone is willing to die rather than to take it back. The cross, for those of Jesus' time, was an instrument of torture and death. For disciples, it is a symbol of radical love. In our own lives, as well, we experience the reality of the Cross. It might look like a child who is terminally ill, a parent with dementia, economic failure, or unemployment. There is no lack of suffering in our lives. The question for the disciple is, "What do we do with the Cross in our path?" Jesus showed us: We lift it up, we carry it, we endure it in faith, and we trust that God will bring good from our willingness to bear it.

Sometimes our cross is found when we try to love those who do not love us in return, or who do not value Gospel love or our attempts to live it, or when we love imperfectly those we have been given to love. If these relationships make God-like love difficult, what are we to do with "enemies"? Is there any way that we can love our enemies when loving our friends and families seems hard enough?

## Who Is Our Enemy?

Can you imagine the disciples when they heard they had to love their enemies? Look into your own heart, and imagine what they felt. Here are men who live in a culture that divides people into castes: high priests, the Roman occupiers, the "unclean," those who conspire with the Romans, prophets, and the rest. They were raised on the Torah with its vision of "an eye for an eye." The disciples must have wondered whether the Teacher was telling them to love the Roman occupiers, their greatest enemy.

At this point in our reflections, we notice that Jesus doesn't give the disciples his whole vision of life in the kingdom of God at once. He takes them one step at a time into union with God, and this teaching on loving their enemies was a difficult step indeed.

Is it really possible to love someone who hates us—who might wish us harm or acts against our well-being? On our own, it isn't possible, but if we examine the life of Christ, we see that his prayer life is what supported his ability to love others. This is the secret ingredient for our own efforts as well.

The paradox in this teaching of Jesus is that the greatest enemy is not the one who will attack us from outside but the one that lurks within our own hearts. It is our fear of all that is not "just like us"—all we cannot control. The truth is that God did not create us to be enemies—but friends and helpmates to each other. God's original vision was of a world of peace where all creatures lived together in right relationship, respected and respecting, true to their own nature and welcoming of those who were different. The garden was not created with only one species of flower or animal. Even God's greatest creation was created "male and female." The unity that God envisioned within the diversity of creation was meant to be embraced and sustained through the unifying grace of God's love embedded in each element of creation. How could that original vision have become so twisted and distorted?

When we look up the word *enemy*, we find that it includes opponents, challengers, rivals, foes, and competitors. Now that's a scary list; it should cause us to pause. It's hard to imagine that we'd consider someone who competes against us as an enemy. Yet with further reflection, competition often involves conflict (both inner and external), and conflict often encompasses discord, disagreement, tension, and even violence. War might be considered the ultimate conflict of rivals and foes who now name each other "enemy."

An honest appraisal of our own behaviors may suggest that we've accepted the conventional wisdom of treating those who disagree with us as though they were enemies—we assault their views; paint them as demons, traitors, or incompetents; and try to "beat them" to achieve our own goals or win others over to our opinions and beliefs. Too many people, including disciples of Christ, are so unconsciously involved in competing with real or imagined enemies that we seldom stop to think about it as an aberration of Gospel love.

## What Is Gospel Love?

If there's any doubt as to what Gospel love looks like, consider Jesus. Jesus' approach to loving others involved:

- Respect
- A listening attitude
- Approachability
- Hospitality
- Nonviolence
- A willingness to heal what is broken in body, mind, or spirit
- A self-sacrificing way of engaging in relationship

Jesus' way of loving crossed the boundaries others imposed, and broke through with the grace of seeing goodness where evil lurked, and offering forgiveness where sin stirred. Jesus didn't just practice Gospel love; he was Gospel love, and he demanded it of his disciples. His words and actions cry out, "Imitate me. Watch what I do when I am persecuted. Listen to my prayer—it embraces all. My heart knows no enemies—and no fear." These are the teachings Jesus offers his disciples then and now—not just in words but even more powerfully in his actions.

The beauty of Jesus' display of Gospel love is that it can be replicated. Everything he did demonstrates for us how we can deal with the enemy within who would impose on us another way.

> Gospel love is the way God showed his love in Jesus.
> It nurtures self-esteem and empowerment.
> It is strong because it is gentle.
> It does not discriminate because of differences.
> Gospel love feeds those who sit at the table
> And invites onlookers to pull up a chair;
> It does not withhold food from the hungry.
> Gospel love quenches the thirst of all who are parched
> And welcomes those who seek refreshment.
> It does not turn away those who yearn for more.
> We were made for Gospel love;
> Created in its image.

## What Does the Story Mean Today?

The third step on the disciple's path focuses us on two verbs: love and pray. It tells would-be disciples that the only way to love our enemies is by praying for them, because prayer changes our own hearts. In step two, we learned that it is in the heart that we learn to live as a blessing—to be poor in spirit, vulnerable, and open to God's grace. In this third step, we reflect on the power of love and prayer to effect this transformation.

In this twenty-first century, it seems like enemies are everywhere. We are surrounded by those we have been taught to fear because they threaten us or who fear us because they sense our aggression toward them or our disdain. Nations gird themselves with weapons; people, with biases. Ideologies ferment distrust and foster superiority. Churches create rules that keep people out—confusing the enemy with those who don't believe in the same way or whose lives fall short of the ideal set out for them.

Every day the media bombards us with images of evil in the form of human belligerence, cruelty, and violence. And in the face of this bombardment, we are often hard pressed to serve up the antidote of Gospel love, if we even think of it. The stories of abhorrent behavior across the globe and down the street abound yet can seem distant from our everyday lives. Yet only glimpses of the sacrifice, generosity, and goodwill millions of people exhibit day after day in the face of unimaginable trials is allowed to break through. As followers of Christ, we are called to be the breakthrough vision of love.

I've known enemies, some very real and others imagined within the heat of disagreement or hurt feelings. In some cases, I've been lied about, deliberately misunderstood, sabotaged, and undermined. I saw those who did these things as my enemies and, in making that distinction, hardened my heart against them. Of course, the result of this heart hardening was to shut down the relationships while declaring far and wide their culpability and my innocence.

Over time, I've seen that naming others as my enemies placed me in a position where I could refuse to look at my own behavior or attitudes. I eliminated my own need to change. I was able to see the splinter in their eyes but not the beam in my own. Because of this, the inner peace that loving your neighbor brings was not just illusive; it was nonexistent. Even when I was blameless, I acted out of pride. Rather than witness to the generous and giving spirit of Jesus, I witnessed instead

to world values that told me to retaliate against anyone who
tried to treat me unjustly—whether in a slight or grievous way.
This is not what brings the heart peace.

Jesus' teaching on love invites us to ponder two types of
enemies:

- those festering within ourselves, that assail us from
  the depths of our own being,

- those that come from the outside, that pummel us
  from within our fractured society.

### Love the enemy within

Who are the very real enemies within? The enemies within
feed on fear and often look like self-centeredness (the fear of
not being enough), greed (the fear of not having enough), dishonesty (the fear of being seen for who we really are), control
(the fear of not getting our way), disrespect for self and others
(the fear of having to live up to our great calling in life), and
inattention to creation (the fear of sacrifice). These enemies rob
us of our ability to see God's glory within ourselves and to use
the power of that glory to transform the face of the earth. The
scriptures tell us that "true love drives out fear" (1 Jn 4:18), so
the fact that we harbor these fears reinforces the work we need
to do in developing the love that resides in the heart of Christ.

Those of us who look at ourselves through eyes blind to our
own goodness or who suffer from low self-esteem also miss the
love of Christ that has taken up residence within us. The ability to offer Gospel love is a sign that we know how much God
loves us. So if we identify a basic inability to love ourselves,
we create a breeding ground for all the other interior enemies.
These look different in each of us, but they hold shared traits.
Those of us who clamor for more, more, and more miss Lazarus, the poor, at our door. Our dissatisfaction with the blessings

in our own lives inhibits our ability to live a life of gratitude and generosity. The emptiness that eats away at our well-being and is meant to be filled with God can never be satisfied with anything other than God's love, which has been given to each of us, in Christ, and which we only need to accept.

Those of us who fear the stranger miss the angel sent to introduce us to God. And our fear of vulnerability, transparency, and authentic relationships defeats our ability to achieve the peace and happiness we so earnestly seek. But when we release the fears we harbor within, we are set free not only to see ourselves through the loving eyes of Christ but also to see others in the same way. The enemy of fear within distorts our understanding of worthiness; freedom from that fear opens our hearts and our lives to the truth of our own worth and empowers us to live out the Gospel love for which we were created.

### Love the enemy that approaches from outside

The enemies outside of us look like war and violence, consumerism, ideological hatred, religious intolerance, nationalism, dehumanization, racism, sexism, jealousy, and revenge—essentially anything that separates us from one another. These enemies prey on our anger at those things we cannot change or control in our lives. They give us a scapegoat—the other. They fill us with a need to strike out, to fill the void of an empty self with false righteousness. Naming others as enemies tells us we are right no matter how many facts show us we are wrong. When we allow these outside enemies to determine how we view life, what we value, or who is worthy, we violate the Lord's great commandments to place God before all idols and to love God with a consuming passion as we love our neighbors as ourselves.

To love our enemies in this third step on the disciple's path is as fresh a teaching today as when the Samaritan decided to help a foreign stranger in need. It is as true as looking in the mirror and seeing there one who needs love, needs prayer, and needs a Savior. We have seen the enemy, and it dwells within just as much as it assails us from outside.

### Pray for those who hate you

Once we've identified the enemies within and outside of us— once we've put a name and a face to them—what comes next?

Our scripture for the third step tells the answer: Pray for those that hate you. Jesus tells us how to achieve Gospel love. We are to turn ourselves over to the power of God and walk in the footsteps of his beloved, Jesus. We are to open our inner being to conversation with God and listen to what God tells us to do. We are to enter into union with the divine One who resides within us and to allow that relationship to form both our conscience and our behavior. For what is prayer but a way to ask and answer the age-old question of the spirit: "Lord, what would you have me do?"

Prayer always brings us an answer, in one form or another. The answer here is to look for what needs changing within us. We hear often, "I want to do God's will." God's will is for us to live the Gospel love of Jesus each and every day, in each and every decision we face. This kind of prayer and action transforms our lives.

Prayer can be our great friend, and the way we come to know God. As our relationship with God deepens, prayer is the fuel that nurtures it and helps us to express our love without fearing consequences. Perfect love casts out fear, the scriptures tell us, and only God is perfect love. It is God's perfect love embodied in Jesus that shows us how to live lovingly in our own lives. Our prayer needs to be a conversation of love, trusting that the Beloved wants only our well-being and happiness and that the path to achieving this promised well-being—while not always straight or easy—is not to be feared.

The disciple's prayer embraces the reality of change and the command to "pick up your cross" in order to accomplish change. The disciple's prayer is all about befriending— changing enemies to friends—befriending what is not whole or Christ-like in us as well as outside of us. The act of befriending implies not accepting evil on its own merit but looking beyond the obvious to what could be and to what was meant to be, re-creating that original vision of God that all creation will live in harmony with its Creator and with all other creatures.

## ☀ Questions
### for Reflection, Journaling, and Discussion

1.  What happens when you use the word "enemies" to identify feelings, qualities, or actions that are part of your life? How would you describe the effect?

2.  Make a list of the enemies that live within you, keeping you from surrender to God. Then make a list of what you perceive as enemies "around" you—those people, events, and ideas that put you on guard and distance you from other humans rather than help you to build God's rule of justice and peace.

3.  How has Jesus spoken to you in this exercise? What does it say about the kind of conversion Christ may be inviting you to consider?

4.  Is your prayer open to conversion, or are you afraid of the sting? What would conversion look like for you in relation to this third step of discipleship—how would you know you were changed?

5.  In what way(s) does your prayer life need to change if it is to become more closely aligned with the prayer and teaching of Jesus and with Gospel love?

## ※ Journal Your Thoughts: May My Heart Be Pure

## A Ritual for Loving Our Enemies

*   Sit very quietly, taking deep breaths.

*   Focus your attention either inwardly with closed eyes or on some particular point on your prayer table (the Bible, a cross, etc.).

*   When you are centered and quiet within, repeat this prayer several times to steady your breathing and deepen your focus: "I am about to walk the very path that you walked, Lord. A lazy person cannot follow this path. May my energy endure. May my prayer be sincere. May my heart be pure."

• Now make a conscious act of dropping all burdens, troubles, or conflicts on the altar of your prayer. Simply turn them over—dump them—on the Lord. With them, put all those people, things, or ideas that you consider your enemies. Visualize yourself dumping them into the prayer pile that is accumulating before you. Let them rest there and then savor the feeling of lightness and peace that comes to you.

• When you are ready, chant/pray:

  * May my enemies be well, happy, and peaceful. May no harm come to them. May no difficulties come to them. May no problems come to them. May they always meet with success. May they also have patience, courage, understanding, and determination to meet and overcome the inevitable difficulties, problems, and failures in life. As I pray for my enemies, I pray for myself and all living beings, in the name of Jesus Christ, my Lord and Savior.
  * Close with the prayer below.

## A Prayer
### for Loving Our Enemies

O Prince of Peace, bless my heart with love for my enemies.

O Christ, in whom I have life, bless my heart with love for my enemies.

O Crucified One, persecuted and killed as an enemy, bless my heart with love for my enemies.

O Resurrected Lord, shining in glory, bless my heart with love for my enemies.

Jesus, Savior of all, let me look on no one as an enemy and may all receive me as a friend. Amen.

# STEP FOUR

# Cultivate a Generous Spirit

D o not judge, and you will not be judged; do not condemn and you will not be condemned. Forgive and you will be forgiven; give and it will be given to you. A good measure, pressed down, shaken together, running over, will be put into your lap; for the measure you give will be the measure you get back.

Luke 6:37–38

## Imagine and Reflect

Here's to all the cheerful givers,
Those whose hand-pocket ratio is celebrated the world over.
Here's to rock stars and models, actresses, and royalty, who
    see a cause and support its success.
Cheers to them—especially if they inspire giving in others.

The rest of us will float in our anonymity
Believing it is not fame that measures the salvific act.
We give as we can—aware our gift won't solve the world's
    problems
Or even those of the family down the street;
Yet hoping that even our feeble attempt to bring justice and
    peace to another
Feeds the life of the world and gladdens the heart of God.

## Love Involves Giving

It is interesting to notice that Jesus inserts his teaching on giving in the midst of his thoughts on not judging or condemning others and just after his teaching on loving our enemies. Obviously the gospel writer means to indicate a correlation, but what is it? Can we imagine giving yet another example of Gospel love? Might it be that giving, as Jesus introduces us to it, is not just about money, but also about opening ourselves to others in such a way that the ordinary barriers of race, differing creeds and ideas, and economic status are no longer formidable? Is it possible that part of the call to be poor in spirit is a refusal to judge or condemn the "poverty" we see in others? As we reflect on this fourth step, let's remember the key verbs that have guided our steps so far: surrender, bless, love, and now, give.

## Entering the Scripture Story:
## Looking for Cheerful Givers

It strikes me that one of my favorite passages, "God so loved the world that He gave his only begotten Son" (Jn 3:16), articulates the right connection between love and giving. God loved so much that he gave what was most precious so that this love could be made real, tangible, and visible to those whom God loved. Because of that generosity, God's love for Jesus and for all creation has been multiplied in the many who have experienced it and who came to understand that they, too, must share it.

Whenever love is authentic and deep, it cannot help but spill out to others. The spillage creates something new, something more. This is what we believe about marriage: When two become one in genuine love that gives fully of itself, new life is possible. Apparently, this is also what Jesus is trying to teach us in this step of our discipleship. When we give fully of the love that has been given to us, it spills over and creates something far beyond our initial gift and certainly beyond our expectations. It creates new life in us and in others.

Similarly, when we withhold our judgments on others and offer instead what they need for new life, we are giving in the way God gives. When we refuse to condemn another because of their weakness, sin, mistakes, or inabilities, we give in the way God gives. I think of story after story in the gospels that show either Jesus giving in this way or applauding others who did: the woman about to be stoned, the widow who gave all she had, the boy with only two loaves and some fish, and the tax collector climbing the tree.

The early followers of the Way understood this teaching on generous giving based on love, at a very basic level. They realized that they were called to take care of each other's needs: to feed the poor; to comfort the widow and orphan who had no one else to stand with them; and to share what they had by giving based on the other's needs, not on their own supply. And when they balked, when they failed to remember the "why" of their giving, their leaders reminded them.

St. Paul coined the phrase "God loves a cheerful giver" (2 Cor 9:7) to motivate the Corinthians, who were not showing a positive attitude on the topic, to donate to the poor in Jerusalem, who were clearly in need.

St. Paul's turn of phrase may seem somewhat naive to our contemporary ears, yet it holds a clear message substantiated by Paul's understanding of the good news of Jesus. Listen as he lays out not just the "why" but also the "how" of generous giving. "The point is this: the one who sows sparingly will also reap sparingly; and the one who sows bountifully will also reap bountifully. Each of you must give as you have made up your mind, not reluctantly or under compulsion, for God loves a cheerful giver. And God is able to provide you with every blessing, in abundance, so that by always having enough of everything, you may share abundantly in every good work" (2 Cor 6:6–8). His thoughts echo Jesus' own words, "Give and it will be given to you . . . with the measure you use, it will be measured to you" (Lk 6:38). He helps us to understand Jesus' message of generosity so that it can penetrate and capture our hearts and flow out into our gifts of time, talent, and treasure for the benefit of others.

### Who is a generous giver?

Most often, people understand that giving of our time, treasure, or talent is a good and noble thing, a "no-brainer." We have only to notice our local communities to witness the good accomplished by those who reach out, with little expectation of reward, to meet human needs and benefit the common good.

I am inspired, for example, by a group of people who come bi-monthly to our parish kitchen to prepare meals that they then serve at a town shelter for the poor and hungry. The meal ingredients and their time and talent are all generously given, without expectation of reward. They motivate me to examine my own giving. But if motivating someone to give were as simple as showing good role models who demonstrate how an ordinary person creatively addresses another's problem, then why doesn't every person step up to the plate of need, as my parish sisters and brothers do, and wipe it clean?

America is one of the most philanthropic countries in the world. Our own citizens couldn't survive without philanthropy, and nonprofit and Church efforts to move us to giving are unending. Efforts like the Peace Corps have reached almost mythic proportions that continue to inspire people of all ages to offer themselves to the less fortunate, expanding beyond the local community or nation of one's birth to embrace those across the globe. With instantaneous communication, we can contribute to the well-being of a family in Africa, Asia, or any continent from our living rooms, doing good from our easy chairs. Yet each worthy global organization is continuously strapped for funds, not to mention workers. How is it that too many hearts remain unmoved? If generosity is so easy, why don't more people give—not from guilt but from a desire to share, and to share cheerfully? After all, isn't sharing cheerfully an act of gratitude?

### Compassion fatigue

One reason we aren't more generous is apparent in the image of "compassion fatigue," that weariness and cynicism that comes when there are just too many causes, too many broken people with their hands out, and too much violence to be undone. There are times when even the most generous dig in their heels and say, "Enough!" "Leave me alone!" "I can't give anything else!" "Let someone else do it!"

Compassion fatigue descends when we can't find the physical, emotional, or spiritual energy to suffer with yet another person. This gradual lessening of compassion over time is easy to recognize. We glaze over when "yet another" media story spotlights starving children. We change the channel that's talking of global warming. When compassion fatigue descends, my desire to give to others becomes a dread of their needs, and the dread leads to withdrawal of time, money, and talent that could be used to make God's love tangible. Even more, compassion fatigue leads me to an inability to experience the joy that comes when I give of myself to feel for and to care for others.

## What are we to do?

Both Jesus and Paul arrive at a bottom-line message: Regardless of how much is asked of us, or how often, we reap what we sow; our own lives will harvest in proportion to what we plant; we are given what we have so that we can use it to benefit others, and generosity should be one of our greatest virtues. When we exercise that virtue motivated by love, we are guaranteed a rich payback, "pressed down, shaken together, running over," and poured into our laps.

As Paul describes the cheerful giver he offers the Corinthians three guidelines for giving that are worth a second look and that help us to determine our "measure."

### Giving needs to be an individual matter

Giving needs to be an individual matter, and each person must make a personal decision and search his or her own heart for the right answer. The rightness of our giving can't be based on what our neighbor gives, nor how guilty we feel, nor what we might have given in the past. Our giving needs to be personal, with the decision coming from an assessment of our own blessings, commitments, and abilities. Our giving needs to be timely, given when needed, not as an afterthought. Each of us is invited to step up—not to rely on others—and to give with a spirit of joyful understanding that God sustains our lives and will not be outdone in generosity. A friend recently mentioned to me that, even though this past year has been very difficult in the face of family problems, and her work has not been good financially, she cannot stop giving her time and resources to help with causes and people in need. She related her great blessings: a great home and land to share, enough food to eat, and time and talent to enter creative ventures. Her sharing reminded me of this teaching of Paul: Our giving will be unique and particular, chosen because we realize our blessings.

### Giving takes commitment and determination to follow through

The Greek verb for giving used in the New Testament (and nowhere else) means "to choose deliberately." So often we give out of emotional response or impulse. Or we say we will give, and then later when we have time to think, we change our minds. Or we commit to service and then fail to show up to do the job. But Paul says this is the wrong way to approach giving. Our giving should be based on a deliberate decision and then followed through with. This implies that giving comes from an inner conviction—even cheerfulness—not whim. Sometimes we allow the difficulties or inconveniences involved in giving to thwart our best intentions, but it doesn't have to be that way. It was inconvenient for Jesus to travel to the grieving sisters of Lazarus, but he did. It must have been difficult for Jesus to offer healing and attention to so many people each day, but he did. He gave, not because he was God and therefore more able than we are, but because he was like us, and, even though he experienced the barriers to full giving, he overcame them by the power of his inner conviction of love and his determination to show that love.

### Giving should be a private offering, not done for publicity

When Haiti suffered its horrific earthquake, donations of money, time, and talent poured in, and that was wonderful and much needed. Yet Haiti has been the poorest county in the Western hemisphere for generations. Perhaps the publicity and acclaim offered to those who made significant donations of money and time made the deciding difference in their giving now rather than in the past. We'll never know, but Jesus' directive to give was like his directive to pray—do so in a way that the left hand doesn't see what the right is doing.

Our generosity of time and talent comes from our poverty of spirit; that is, affirming that all we have comes from God. It comes from our response to Christ's call, our continued openness to our brother and sister in need—yes, even our enemies in need. Even though our country is seen as an enemy by some other countries, it does not stop us from giving when they experience severe catastrophes and people are suffering. Our country, as we ourselves, must give not from a sense of guilt but from a sense of solidarity with others who are our brothers and sisters. When we give in this way, we turn our private act, our personal or corporate response, into a building stone for the kingdom of God. It becomes a gift of life that energizes not only our own spirit but also those who receive and those who witness it.

### Generosity is nonnegotiable for disciples

Both Jesus and Paul tell us that, to follow Christ, generosity is nonnegotiable. It isn't a matter of giving or not giving but how best to give based on what has been given to us. Paul tells us further that there are four beneficiaries of our giving: the giver, the recipients, God, and the Church. Let's unpack this a bit.

### We are the first beneficiary of our giving

Our giving is blessed with "abounding grace," and this grace can be seen not just in life's material blessings but also the spiritual riches that come from being in union with God's will. This grace takes the form of inner strength and power that flows from trusting in God's providence and promise to take care of our needs. It feels like inner freedom where we find the ability to freely give of what we have and who we are and are not limited by our fear of having less. Instead, we are exhilarated with the realization of God's abundance and how we share in that. As we learn to be content with what we have and to live based on our needs rather than on our wants, we find that we have more awareness of others' needs and more ability to supply those needs. It's mysterious at times as to how this all works, but we know this: It works to our good and contributes to our growth as good people.

### The recipients of our generosity benefit

They are reminded that God is watching over them through those who care for them. They see the Gospel come alive as those who follow Christ take seriously his teachings. They see a model that they, themselves, can follow. Each of us, regardless of our means or talents, is asked to give in order to help others meet their necessities. Even the poor have much to offer, as the widow in the gospels, who gave all she had, understood.

As recipients of our generous care, concern, and generosity, others are reminded that they too can affect the life of another. Perhaps they will do it not with material giving but through listening, kind acts, peaceful interaction, and much more; each can give new life. This is another benefit for when the poor give to us we realize that it isn't just material things that count as Gospel giving, often, that is the least important thing.

### God is the third beneficiary of our generosity

At first glance, this may seem an odd thought. Yet, when someone gives generously, without fanfare and because it flows from the desire to please God and to follow Christ, then the gratitude and praise of the recipients can be directed toward God, and together giver and receiver can give glory to God, the giver of all good things. God has no need of our generosity, but God does desire our praise and thanks. God does want us to acknowledge that what we do is inspired by what God does, that is, gives generously out of love. I think here of something I read in an interview with Mother Teresa who told the story of a dying man, filled with sores and disfigured, who was being lovingly tended by one of the Sisters of Charity. He asked her, "Why are you doing this?" She answered, "Because I love you." He said, "How can you love me? We are strangers." She said, "I love you because Jesus loves you, and because of Jesus' love, we are not strangers but family." In her simple way, she helped that non-Christian man to raise his eyes and his heart to God, to give God glory.

### Finally, the Church benefits when we are generous

Through the generous giving of its members, the Church itself is reminded that God is alive and working in our midst. The immediate result of generous giving might be a particular financial goal reached or a particular job completed; but the ultimate benefit is that the Church, the People of God, is refocused on God's abundant and generous love and we are challenged once again to understand that faith and good works walk hand in hand and it is our responsibility to live out our faith by generously giving.

## What Does the Story Mean Today?

Reading the gospels from any angle finds Jesus demonstrating generosity: giving of his time as he listened to countless concerns and pleas for help; sharing the little he had, like a meal of bread and fish, praise for the woman who bathed his feet with oil and the widow who gave all she had; and offering his talent by speaking words of wisdom and comfort, healing people physically and spiritually, and presenting a hospitable spirit, friendship, and support in hard times. His giving drew others to be with him and to imitate his generosity with their own.

Jesus did not begrudge what he gave. Wherever he came upon need, he reached out. Like all of us, the energy it took to be attentive to the needs around him drained him. When "compassion fatigue" threatened to set in, Jesus withdrew to prayer and the support of his closest disciples.

Look to prayer and support when you need it—what a novel idea! Learning from Jesus, we find three tools that today's disciples can use to energize their generosity:

- prayer,
- small Christian community,
- and radical trust in God's care and protection.

## Prayer

The kind of prayer Jesus engaged in when his compassion was lagging and his generosity had hit a roadblock was contemplation. He took himself apart to a quiet place, centered himself on God's presence, and opened his heart radically to God's care and protection, fully expecting to receive a dose of God's generosity and a renewal of body, mind, and spirit. Contemplative prayer is similar to meditation but without the outside prompts like a scripture reading or a visualization formula. In contemplative prayer, we bring our whole selves to a place of quiet encounter where we await the experience of God's presence. In contemplative prayer we set ourselves before God, alert and waiting, neither troubled nor anxious to make it happen, simply glad to be with the beloved, allowing heart to speak to heart.

Contemplative prayer looks easy because there is no need for special tools, words, places, or knowledge. Yet, to our busy, verbal, Western mind, it seems a foreign exercise. It's actually an ancient form of prayer that is an integral part of the Christian tradition. To engage in contemplative prayer is to focus our whole being on God, knowing that God is focusing on us. There is no agenda, no seeking of answers, and no "product." We attempt to "be" and allow the Holy Spirit to speak the desire we don't even know is within us.

In contemplation, in the deep breathing of prayer and a quiet surrounding devoid of phone, TV, computer, or other stimuli, our hearts quiet and our resistance weakens, because, as we place our resistance into the heart of God, we experience God's reserve of compassion that fills us with hope and energy. Heart to heart with God, we are renewed.

## Small Christian community

Gathering with a small group to intentionally support and challenge one another to greater discipleship is not a new spiritual discipline. Rather, it is a renewed form of "being the Church" that Catholic Christians are rediscovering. In a world that prizes competition and the isolated interaction of a keyboard, deciding to join with others to be known and to know for the sake of better understanding and living God's will for our lives can have us feeling vulnerable. Yet for those who sincerely desire to grow in their discipleship, and to bring the world into the reign of God, there is no better alternative.

Belonging to a small Christian community provides a framework for reading and sharing the scripture, an avenue of accountability to lessen the possibility of ignoring God's voice or "backsliding" on goals and promises to change, a loving support system to help us negotiate the difficult times in life, and a ready-made party list of those who will rejoice in every triumph no matter how small.

In a small Christian community, our decisions for generous giving find support. We are challenged by both the spiritual life of the group and the witness of others.

Even Jesus needed a small Christian community to support his spiritual journey. He found it in the group of men and women he gathered around him and who walked with him day in and day out, in good or difficult times. It was his small community that marveled at his healing power, prayed with him throughout Galilee and Judea, shared his last meal, gathered in the upper room to mourn and make sense of his tragic death, and rejoiced at the empty tomb.

If our hearts are to grow in a generosity that allows us to stretch even to laying down our lives for our friends, this kind of support is what we need.

## Radical trust in God's providence

The third thing we learn from Jesus' form of generous living and unending compassion, and Paul's challenge to cheerful giving, is that it cannot be done by human desire alone.

Compassion that doesn't get tired of giving, generosity that does not reach a limit, is not something that is controlled by the will; it is fostered and maintained by faith and trust in God's own compassion and generosity. If ever we need a role model, we have only to recount that God "gave his only Son" in a supreme act of generous love.

It is not our goodwill that feeds the poor but the goodwill of God acting through us. It is not our compassion that heals a wounded spirit but the compassion of God living in our words and actions. In union with God, we find the internal resources to transform our external circumstances. In trusting that God will never fail us, we surrender the need to acquire more at the cost of others' lives.

I will never forget a profound example of this that touched my own life and still acts as a lodestar of trust. Several years ago, when my husband was volunteering one year of his life to help our diocese establish a sister relationship with a diocese in the Dominican Republic, we traveled several times to that island nation, to meet and serve the people and to assess needs, resources, and challenges. On one particular occasion, we traveled several hours from the capital over hot, dusty, bumpy mountain roads to one of the provincial towns and, from there, several more hours, in even more extreme conditions, to a very small hamlet of eight homes identified as in need of assistance.

We pulled into the complex, hot and sweaty, tired and sore, and aware of the caution not to drink the water. The scene before us was incredible. There were eight very tiny, stick-built homes, with thatched roofs and dirt floors, homes with openings but no windows or doors. The community of families gathered outside to greet us with shy smiles and a warm welcome. We were invited to enter their homes. The home I entered housed a family of six. It had one twin mattress, a small wooden table, and two chairs, one of which had a shortened leg that made it wobble. That was it.

The woman who invited me into her home did so with pride and such a generous spirit that I was almost overcome. When I asked her where her children slept, she pointed to the mattress. When I asked where she and her husband slept, she indicated that they slept on the dirt floor. When I noted that this must be a hardship for them, she nodded but said, "No es importa, porque Dios nos da todo que necesitamos." (It isn't important, because God gives us everything we need.)

This simple woman humbled me with her faith, her trust in God's providence, and her generous hospitality to me, a stranger. Whenever I am tempted to mistrust God's care or to be reluctant to give, I think of her, my sister—a cheerful giver who gave abundantly from the little she had.

### Life of abundance or life of scarcity?

The path less traveled in this fourth step is the path of the abundant life—living the quality of generosity whose source is the overflowing generosity of God.

Jesus taught that he came that we might have life "and to have it abundantly" (Jn 10:10).

That sets the direction for the goal and reward of discipleship: live from an experience of abundance. The challenge is to leave behind those who have translated the meaning of that abundance into material things, confusing the "good life" with what Jesus calls "abundant life." This jaundiced understanding of abundance has no place on the disciple's path; it will not bring peace, joy, or wholeness. It is really a perspective of scarcity that depicts the neighbor as a threat and giving as a diminishment of security. The truth is that God's generosity is a higher call. It gives beyond what is deserved or expected without concern for repayment, praise, or reward, and is demonstrated throughout the scriptures and our own lives.

We find this theology of abundance in a traditional Passover song, "Dayenu," sung for over a thousand years, which begins, "How many levels of favors has the Omnipresent One bestowed upon us." Then as the lyrics tell the Passover story, each line of history is completed with the word Dayenu, "It would have been enough." "If He had brought us out from Egypt, and had not carried out judgments against [the oppressor] . . . Dayenu! If He had destroyed their idols and had not smitten their first-born . . . Dayenu!"

But God never gives simply enough; God does more than "we can desire or pray for." This is the abundance God shows us, and this is the "living from abundance" that graces the life of the disciple who has met the living God, in Jesus Christ. It is this disciple who gives cheerfully, realizing that whatever he or she gives will never be enough to repay so gracious and generous a God.

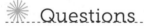 ## Questions

### for Reflection, Journaling, and Discussion

1. Do you live life as though you believe in abundance or scarcity? What's one thing you can do to live more abundantly?

2. Name some of the ways in which God's abundance has overflowed into your life. How might you "pass it forward" to another?

3. Describe a time when you experienced cheerful giving. In your experience, how does that happen?

4. Have you ever received more than you have given? In what ways has your generosity been rewarded?

5. Of the three resources for cultivating generosity of spirit: contemplation, small Christian community, and radical trust in God's care, which are you now practicing, and which might you try to bring into your life more fully? How and when will you begin?

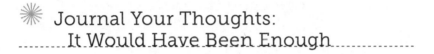

## ✳ Journal Your Thoughts:
..........It Would Have Been Enough..............

## Ritual Actions for Those Seeking a More Generous Heart

- Create a gratitude list, and add to it every day; celebrate those things for which you are grateful, for instance, friendships, family, good health, beauty, and community.

- Join or form a small Christian community of those dedicated to the disciple's path who will encourage and challenge you to generous giving.

- Make small changes to your daily consumption, living more simply and sharing your "wealth" in whatever form, with those less fortunate.

- Begin to write your life story, listening to it for the tales of holiness and of God's abundance.

- Write your own Dayenu prayer, thinking of the many blessings God has poured into your life, giving you far more than "enough." For example, "If God had only given me good parents, Dayenu."

## Prayer

### of the Cheerful Giver

O God, if you had given me only the song of the birds and the warmth of the sun, Dayenu!

O God, if you had only allowed me one person to love me in my life, Dayenu!

O God, if you had measured my days in months and hours, Dayenu!

I seek to serve you, O loving and generous God, for your graciousness gives me the power to give to others with a cheerful and contented heart.

I seek to praise you, O loving and generous God, for the bountiful blessings you have given and the never-ending love that you offer.

I seek to thank you, O loving and generous God, for the gifts of life, love, and joy that you never cease to give me in my Lord, Jesus Christ. Amen.

## STEP FIVE

# Pray
# Like
# Jesus

I call to you, LORD, come quickly to me; hear me when I call to you. Let my prayers rise like incense in your sight; the lifting of my hands like an evening oblation.

Psalm 141

## Imagine and Reflect

I don't need words to reach your heart,
Gentle and loving One,

For when you stepped into my being with your precious love
You filled me to overflowing with your presence.
You lit the coals of praise and worship in my spirit
And ignited my passion to renew the earth.

77

The fire that you lit in my soul
Has not diminished.
It roars with the heat of your love
And an openness to all that lives.

Now I find you everywhere,
In all things your presence abounds
—a gentle breeze
—the rubble aftermath of earthquakes and hurricanes
—the laughter of children
—folded flags in the arms of grieving families
—the sun melting dew from the grass
—fading light in the eyes of the dying
—a whisper in the recesses of my heart
—that calm, empty space that only you can fill

I don't need words to reach your heart,
Gentle and loving One

## Prayer Is Not about Words

Too often we think prayer is about words. We may even think
prayer is about a certain way of saying the words, of using only
the "correct" words. In our efforts to be precise and correct and
to follow all the rules about prayer, we can lose its essence and
end up wondering why our time with God seems sterile, dry,
or unsatisfying.

Have you ever listened to a small child at prayer? Their
words flow freely and are not self-conscious. They pour out
their hearts with the simple trust that the prayer will be heard.
What happened to us along the way from birth until now?
How did our easy childlike way of being with God and spill-
ing our hearts out change into formal and ritualistic patterns?
Who told us that in order to pray we had to fold our hands a

certain way, be in a certain place, or use a certain book? Why did we believe them? Why are we still so slow to grasp the truth of our own hearts?

### Prayer is about being connected to the love of our lives

It's about allowing our whole being—body, mind, and spirit— to rest at peace in the presence of the One who loves us. It's about claiming our heritage as God's beloved and pouring into God's lap the entirety of who we are or have ever wanted to be. Prayer is a spoken or unspoken love letter that holds nothing back, that has no fear of the intimacy of honest sharing, and that allows our own vulnerable selves to be exposed to the knowing and loving gaze of the loved One.

### Prayer is as much about offering love as receiving it

So prayer is also about being quiet, ceasing the word flow, stopping the mind from thinking, and simply opening our hearts to receive the love that God seeks to wash over us.

### Prayer is dangerous because it changes us

Prayer isn't about changing God or God's plan for the world. It's about soaking in all that God love so that we can change those parts of ourselves that are still ego driven, still self-centered, and still godless. Maybe that's why we don't pray as we should or as often; change can be a frightening possibility. Yet as we learned in step three, when we overcome the enemies from within, we are freed to receive the blessings that God wants to give.

This fifth step of our disciple's walk is epitomized with the verb "pray." Taking this step will cause us to slow down, to evaluate the worth of our busyness, and to reprioritize our time with God to the top of our "to do" lists. More than being about prayer in a generic sense, our fifth step will help us to recapture the way that Jesus prayed, to pray the dangerous prayer that transforms not only our lives but also our relationship with God and others.

## Entering into the Scripture Story: Qualities of the Prayer of Jesus

### Jesus' life and his prayer were one, rising like incense to praise God

When we look at the gospels' portrayal of Jesus, we can easily see that his life was a prayer, an ongoing expression of his relationship with God that led to his inner conversion and his life of service to others. Jesus embodied his prayer; his love, praise, trust, and gratitude in God wasn't something he thought about. It was something that flowed through him, like the air we breathe, like the smoke of incense.

The first recorded use of incense in worship was with the Egyptians, two thousand years before the birth of Christ. Since that time, every known religious tradition has incorporated incense, in some form, into its worship. Further developed in China and spread throughout Asia, incense is an important element in Asian religious traditions and in Buddhist ceremonies as well. It is used to purify surroundings, objects, and participants.

In Christianity, incense has been used since the early days of the Church, especially in the Eastern Rite Churches and in the high sacramental churches like Roman Catholicism. Some scholars believe that the use of incense in prayer and worship comes from the earlier traditions of Judaism around the time of the Second Temple and is rooted in Psalm 141, "Let my prayer rise like incense, in your sight; the lifting up of my hands as an evening sacrifice." In the Roman (Latin) tradition, incense is offered in waves of three to remind us of the Holy Trinity: Father, Son, and Holy Spirit. In the book of Revelation, the referral to incense is meant to symbolize the prayers of the saints in heaven.

So, in all faith traditions, from ancient times to the present, we hear the call to visualize our prayers rising to God as incense, like smoke that wafts and floats, that cleanses the air of impurities, and that lifts itself effortlessly, roaming where it will and not giving a second thought once it is sent to the Holy One.

That's how our childhood prayer was. That's how Jesus' prayer was. That's how our prayer needs to be again, not self-conscious and rigidly correct, but effortless: heart speaking to heart without fear of consequences; floating freely in the presence of the Other; unafraid and unashamed; and wanting only to offer love, praise, and gratitude and to receive in return an experience of union, unquestioning hope, and clarity of purpose.

## Leaping, listening, obeying, noticing, pondering, and resting

One way to describe Jesus' prayer is to compare it to the smoke that rises from incense, but what other images do the gospels give us to describe prayer?

We are told that in his mother's womb Jesus **"leapt for joy."** Here we see that Jesus' prayer was embodied, not just a system of words but leaping from his very being. As a child, he sat with the scholars to learn of God, and what he learned of God led to **obedience to God's voice** found in the concern, questions, and instruction of his parents. So his prayer was the **prayer of study and discernment**. What he learned was that merely knowing God's will is not enough; we must also act on God's will. Our prayer must move us to obedience to the God we come to know in our prayer. Jesus went regularly to the synagogue for **communal sharing of the sacred scriptures**. He knew that in the Torah he would learn the identity of the God to whom he prayed.

Jesus also blessed God **as he reflected on nature**, using natural references frequently to call attention to God's active presence. Being a good Jew, Jesus was aware of the many references to nature in the Torah, as well as the Jewish holistic view that pointed to a creation permeated with the presence of its Creator. He talked of sheep, fig trees, wheat, water, chickens, mud, birds, and more, realizing how well these natural elements spoke to the real experience of his listeners. Is there any wonder that so many people say they feel closest to God in nature? That being in nature *is prayer* for them?

Jesus sought out **places and times of solitude for contemplative prayer** when he was wearied by the crowds, when he needed time to discern God's will, and when he was in desolation and sought God's consolation. He knew the power of **silent prayer** as he stood before the judgment of the crowds and of Pilate; and he knew the **prayer of words** to convey his final prayer on the Cross for others and himself.

Jesus' entire life can be understood from the vantage point of his prayerful stance before God and reveals a deep intimacy with God sustained by faith and trust.

There is a tendency in some to dismiss the humanness of Jesus' prayerful walk through life by pointing out that he was God's Son and therefore we should expect him to be intimate with God and to approach life in the way he did. Certainly, it is understandable to think this. However, it is also heretical, since the Church has taught clearly since the Council of Nicaea that Jesus was *both* God *and* man, *neither* of which overcomes or dominates the other. Jesus lived his humanity and divinity in perfect harmony. His Incarnation teaches us that we, too, are called to this harmonic balance: our humanity in harmony with our infused life of God, in Christ.

Our prayer, in the Spirit of Jesus, is to be embodied. In prayer we allow ourselves to leap with joy, to commune with nature, to obey God's voice, to discern our purpose, and to respond in service. But how do we begin?

### Imitation is the highest form of praise

How are we to imitate so great a love and intimacy as displayed by Jesus with his Abba? Who are we to believe we can reach such profound connection with our God?

We hear our hearts proclaim, "Jesus, your very birth was an act of wonder and awe at the powerful works of God. You never failed to seek your Father's counsel, or to trust your Father's wisdom. When you were lost, you found refuge in the house of your Father. Your ministry radiated 'Abba,' who gave you strength and guidance. Your suffering and death were wrapped in a state of holy contemplation. You brought fire upon the earth and kindled it first within your own heart. This fire of love was the source of your power to heal others and the world. Its roaring flames consumed your own life, and you have passed it forward into ours. How are we to imitate so great a love?"

## The Prayer of Jesus

Of all the teaching Jesus offers us in the scriptures, his teaching on prayer is most profound in its simplicity just as it is most revolutionary in its content. Jesus must have understood that to move away from formulaic prayers and into the prayer of the heart (embodied prayer) might be a difficult or frightening thing for his disciples and, ultimately, for us. So in his caring way, he taught us how to pray.

### Our Father

All of us are familiar with the prayer that begins, *Our Father, who art in Heaven*. The first thing we notice in this prayer is that Jesus approaches God in an inclusive way, demonstrating that God is not the exclusive possession of any one person or group of believers. God belongs to all and is in all, thus, "our" Abba. To approach God as one who cannot be defined by individual biases, beliefs, or lack of imagination is to allow God the power to rule over our lives and not be imprisoned by any imposed boundaries. "Our" father, our Abba, is the one who created and loves all.

Jesus calls his father "Abba," meaning daddy, a term that reveals God's desire to be known intimately—not as an impersonal parent figure with rules and laws, but as a loving, approachable daddy, whose discipline is loving and whose love is unconditional. There are people for whom the word "father" is anything but a reminder of love. They have a hard time relating to God as Father. But Jesus removes harshness, formality, or distance by using the word "Abba," not a term he was taught in school or synagogue perhaps, but a name that came from his own relationship. By naming God in this way, he honored his own experience of God and gave us permission to name God as we experience God, not just in the ways that have been handed down to us. In addition to Jesus' use of the parenting image for God that we all understand, he also used other endearing impressions: of a hen who gathers her babies around her for protection and a woman who cannot forget the child of her womb. These, among other metaphors, solidify his understanding of this God of intimacy and inclusiveness and enrich our own imagining of who God can be for us.

### Who are in Heaven, holy Is your name

The next lesson we learn in the Our Father is that where the fullness of God's rule exists, wherever God reigns in holiness, is called heaven. Heaven is not simply some gathering of clouds in the sky; it the place where the fullness of God resides. In heaven, all those who see God face to face and know God more intimately than they could ever have imagined obey God and do God's will with pure joy. They come to meet God, eager to obey and eager to praise God day and night. This is what the kingdom of God is like, and this is what we are commanded to bring about in our own lives, beginning with and accomplished through prayer.

Our call to create the reign of God is all about fashioning environments and relationships where God rules, including within us. We see God face to face in Jesus, and so as we acquire a deeper relationship with Christ, we are strengthened for the task of building and gain wisdom to know how best to live as kingdom people.

In order to honor God's holy name, we have to live with the humility to know our place in the presence of the Master, a process that is another name for prayer.

### Your Kingdom come, Your will be done on earth as it is in heaven

Here we see why the Our Father is revolutionary, why it calls the disciple to conversion. Jesus doesn't want his disciples to live in "future" attentiveness to God's will. He wants us to create a world in which God rules now, to make heaven on earth today. What would the earth look like if God's will ruled? Would starving people still exist? Would nations be locked in warfare? Would greed, pettiness, and meanness of spirit be alive and powerful? I think not.

It's easy to fall into the trap of reading these words and thinking in great, abstract terms, while failing to bring this understanding back to the streets where we live. When we pray "your kingdom come, your will be done," we are doing two things: yearning for the final time of bliss when God is all for all and accepting that this in-between time in which we live is the soil in which we are called to work so that all people can experience a glimpse of that time to come in their lives now. We catch these glimpses of kingdom living every time we bring nonperishable goods to our parish food baskets, attend interfaith prayer services for peace, or refuse to be drawn into harsh words that condemn, ridicule, or judge others. We get a taste of the kingdom to come each time we dine at the table of the Lord and are fed with our God, sit at the bedside of the sick and pray for their healing, or experience the kindness of others when we are in distress.

This is God's will: That we, God's beloved, live the deepest, most generous desires of our own hearts—that very place where God resides. It is here that we will find the path of peace and abundance that dances to the will of God. It is in this way that we will make God's will as real on earth as it is in heaven. And this is what prayer does and what the prayer of Jesus teaches us.

## Give us our daily bread

Here Jesus proclaims trust in God's providence and care, faith that God will provide what we need to meet the situations of each day. Daily we are to call upon the Lord, and daily God will provide what feeds our body, mind, and spirit.

The dailyness of prayer cannot be overemphasized. Jesus is telling us not to take God for granted but to place before God, each day, our needs. What is that bread that we need? The word "bread" may be taken literally, as the basic food for our bodies. Bread is food, but it also symbolizes other basic needs like clothing and shelter. Bread, like manna, is God's gift, and by teaching us to ask for it, we are reminded that we depend on God's goodness for our very survival—that everything, even the necessities of life, depend less on our own efforts and more on God's generosity.

## Forgive us as we forgive others

This forgiveness Jesus prays for has a sting. Will God forgive us? Yes—in the manner we forgive others. Ouch! Some prefer forgiveness that will not change their lives. But if we pray in the manner of Jesus, then Pilate is forgiven, a blaspheming thief is forgiven, the crowd that condemns can be forgiven, and even an intimate betraying friend is worthy of forgiveness—for they do not know what they do. To pray as Jesus did transforms the heart into one that forgives, one that mirrors the forgiveness of God.

If forgiveness seems beyond what is humanly possible, perhaps that's because it is. Without claiming the power of God and surrendering our own desire to withhold our forgiveness as a form of revenge or self-indulgence, we cannot forgive. God is merciful, but God is also just. This prayer shows us that, when we ask for forgiveness from God, God's mercy will forgive us even before we ask; but God's justice considers how well we exercise our own power to forgive.

## Deliver us from evil

This petition brings us full circle. Jesus asks Abba for protection from falling prey to choices, actions, situations, people, and ideologies that are not in tune with God's rule, God's will, and God's way. Without divine help we are capable of straying from our best intentions, putting God aside and choosing what contradicts God's way. Jesus' prayer doesn't ask to be spared from evil but to be delivered—not to be engulfed by its lure.

Evil definitely exists, and this petition acknowledges that: Deliver us from evil, the wicked one, the tempter. Here we pray that the evil that surrounds us will not overwhelm us and, more, that we will not participate in spreading evil, that we will refuse to extend evil's influence in the world.

## What Does the Story Mean Today?

When I talk with spiritual direction clients or clients in pastoral counseling, I usually ask them to describe their prayer lives. After the first few stammering attempts, many will say, "Well, I don't really have time for much prayer. I try to pray while I'm driving to work, or maybe once a week I can fit in some prayer time." The conversation, needless to say, turns to why it's so important not to just say prayers or fit prayers into our busy schedules but also to become living prayer, in the manner of Jesus. One suggestion I sometimes give to help people who grapple with this challenge is to suggest that they create a cloister in their hearts. After a few startled seconds, the conversation continues to unpack what that means.

## A Cloister in the Heart

Creating a cloister in our hearts isn't about joining a monastery; it's about acquiring the characteristics that made monks true reformers as well as proclaimers of the Word. It's about honoring God's own advice, "Be still and know that I am God" (Ps 46:10). It's remembering that discipleship and discipline are from the same root word, pointing us to the fact that, once we have committed to following Christ, we need to find the discipline that will allow us to remain faithful to that choice. It is creating a still, quiet place within that makes room for God, a space where God can communicate. It is in this interior place that we will come to know the purpose of our lives and find the courage to live it with passion. This is how we live the prayer of Jesus today. This is how we find the vision and the strength that Jesus found to make God's name holy, to seek and obey God's will, to rely on God's providence, to extend God's mercy, and to reject what is not of God.

We are able to walk the disciple's path because we pray, because we have created that sacred inner place of quiet and union with God in prayer. In the Church's early history, monks and nuns were cloistered; they lived apart from the world. They gathered in walled communities where they set up a daily routine for physical and spiritual survival. They were single-minded, able to endure physical, emotional, and spiritual hardships, and willing to embrace both a life of solitude and the uncontrollable idiosyncrasies of life in community, each of which empowered them to service and sacrifice. This, too, was in the manner of Jesus.

## The Power of the Cloistered Heart

Unlike the walled cloisters of eras past, the cloister in our hearts is unwalled; open to the world and designed for action. Our hearts have no need for walls, imitating the heart of Christ who placed no barriers between himself and the world. This cloister image offers interesting characteristics that are epitomized in the prayer of Jesus and remain relevant today as we continue to learn to pray in the manner of Jesus:

- Prayer needs time and an attitude that is based on humility, self-sacrifice, obedience to God's will, and service of others.

- Prayer is both a relationship and a discipline that feeds our desire for holiness and wholeness.

- Prayer is a commitment to life in community, to share ourselves and to work alongside others to achieve common goals.

- Prayer is living within a daily rhythm of inner stillness, community, and work.

- Prayer is a vow, a promise to restore the reign of God.

- Prayer is being in love and allowing that love to drive our choices.

- Prayer is the fuel that rekindles the fire of the Spirit within us so that we have the stamina and courage to throw that fire before us wherever we go.

These representations of prayer will never be realized unless we adopt three elements that act as building blocks for the creation of our inner cloister:

- embracing solitude,

- engaging in community,

- and committing to service and the transformation of the world.

This is what Jesus' prayer empowered him to do. This is what praying in the manner of Jesus inspires disciples who follow him to do.

## Solitude

Early disciples went to the desert as hermits as an antidote to a church and world that were not living up to the ideal. They sought solitude and silence both as penance for all that was wrong with the world and as a way to empty themselves of the distractions and noise that blotted out the voice of God. What they found was a sacred presence so profound that they were inspired to open their hearts and their hermitages to others in genuine acts of hospitality, healing, and solidarity.

These many years later, the world is still chaotic and the noise has only increased. We need solitude and quiet as much as any ancient hermit in order to know ourselves as God knows us and to hear, in the deepest recesses of our hearts, who God is asking us to become. Solitude, that is, periods of aloneness and quiet, is where we meet God most profoundly. It is where we have space and time to listen to our experiences in the context of God's presence. It is free from the noise of our own thoughts and the thoughts of others with whom we live and work. Solitude is what Jesus sought so that he could listen to God.

It isn't always easy to sit alone, in silence, wondering if God will speak. But it is the foundation for forming our hearts on the heart of Christ, for developing our desire for community, and for planting and watering the seeds of our call to ministry.

### Community

In one of his works, Henri Nouwen taught that solitude always leads to community. I agree, but it isn't necessarily the community as experienced in groups in formal organizations. The community we are called to from our solitude is a way of life, a deep, authentic engagement with family, friends, groups of the heart, and purpose.

In community we realize that we are one small part of something much larger, one of many who are beloved of God. In community we learn to see and love God in all the diversity that God is; we learn to see ourselves in union with others, moving forward toward some common destiny that, alone, we cannot achieve.

We know that living in community—whether family, church, work, or intentional communities of faith—isn't easy. Someone once said, "Community is that place where the person you least want to live with, lives." I've lived in several forms of community over my lifetime, and each required of me qualities I didn't know I had until they were challenged: leadership, humility, forgiveness, and perseverance. I learned who I am and who God is thanks to others with whom I lived in community. I still learn through my interactions in my parish community; my volunteer work with neglected and abused children and the other staff members and volunteers with whom I have joined to make a difference; the joys, sorrows, and tensions of family life; and the cyclical movement of relationships.

Why is solitude the foundation for community? Because without learning to know ourselves in the mystery of God's love and to know that in God alone will we find what we need to fulfill our purpose in life, then we will seek our identity and purpose in other people and in other places. We'll be more vulnerable to the opinions and influence of others whether or not those others lead us more deeply into union with God. We need our solitude to make sense of our community experience, and our community experience to give substance to our solitude and motivation for our service.

## Service and world transformation

Jesus modeled for us, both in his prayer and in his life, the importance of solitude and community. He went often to a quiet place so that he could discern God's will and find the inner resources he needed to accomplish it. He gathered others around him, in community, to share his life, his vision, his faith, and his work. The prayer of Jesus and the purposeful engagement with others led him naturally to service. This needs to be our pattern as well.

We are each called to the *diakonia* typified by the early disciples. It is God-like to be of service to others. Within the cloisters of our hearts, we hear God's compelling direction and we feel the affirmation of God's love. Among our communities of faith, family, and service, we see the faces of those who need the love we have to give and who validate our reason for giving it. These alternating rhythms ignite our desire to reach out in service to a world that continues to need transformation if the reign of God is to be fully established.

Service takes so many forms, yet the Second Vatican Council teaches that the laity's first focus for service needs to be in transforming the world through our work, our families, and our civic institutions. This is where we can make the greatest inroads for Christ. This is where we have a unique entry point and unlimited power and influence for good. This is where we create a world of peace and a society of justice. We are called to make a difference, whether small or great, wherever we are.

I could describe a laundry list of service opportunities that would only serve to illustrate what we all readily know: The ways to serve are endless. Instead, I am inspired by a line attributed to Blessed Teresa of Calcutta, great servant of God, who not only lived in community but also spent three or more hours every day in prayer, and who points out that "prayer in action is love, and love in action is service." When our hearts are in tune with the love of God for us and ours for God, and our community is rich in its desire to know, love, and serve God, then our love overflows in service of those in need and all are blessed.

We began this chapter reflecting on the truth that Jesus did not just pray; he became prayer, that is, a sacred offering to his Abba, united as one with his God and all others. We close this chapter remembering that our cloistered hearts beat a rhythm of praying and working according to the hours of the day, stopping regularly in the midst of all that seems so important to give undivided attention to God. We are challenged to let ourselves stop—as though we have heard the monastery bell, as if we saw others drop their work to walk to the chapel, and as though we had no other care than to be with the beloved. We are invited to allow a warm breeze to call us to prayers of praise; a person's distress, to prayers of petition and comfort; and our weariness, to gratitude. The life of the world brings energy to our still, unwalled hearts, pumping the Christ life within us forward into a needy world.

It is through our cloistered hearts, engaged in community and active in service, that we will offer others the following:

- A quiet refuge of kind thoughts and peaceful emotions

- A place of welcome for all who need courage, solace, or rest

- A den of hospitality that knows no strangers and recognizes unlikely angels

- A harbor of deep connection to God

- A companion in the pursuit of justice

- A font of compassion

And with this, step five also asks us to wonder,

What if each disciple prayed like Jesus?
Would the blind see, the deaf hear, the lame walk?
Would people stop killing each other and live in peace?

Would the earth be restored to its fullness,
And all have enough to be full and happy?

What if each disciple prayed as Jesus did?

Would God's name again be honored and idols crushed?

Would heaven permeate earth?

Would forgiveness be a way of life

And each person's hand outstretched to bless?

What if each disciple prayed like Jesus?

 Questions

## for Reflection, Journaling, and Discussion

1. What is there about the Our Father that is a source of "conversion" for you?

2. Can you relate to the image of making a cloister in your heart? Would you describe your prayer life as a rhythmic harmony of prayer and work? How could you make this a reality?

3. The crux of prayer is to change the heart of the one who prays and to create an urgency or passion for justice and service. Does your prayer do this? What can you do to open your heart to this type of prayer?

4. What if you prayed like Jesus? What would happen in your life? How would it affect your service in the world?

 Journal Your Thoughts: Abba

## A Ritual for Praying the Prayer of Jesus

Pray the prayer of Jesus aloud, using both your body and your voice:

> Our Father, Who Are in Heaven
> > (Arms extended in front with palms up, reaching for God)
> Holy Is Your Name
> > (Arms/hands crossed over your heart and head bowed)
> Your Kingdom Come, Your Will Be Done, on Earth as It Is in Heaven
> > (Arms extended in front, circling in a gathering motion, then pointing to the earth, and then up again toward the sky)
> Give Us Today Our Daily Bread
> > (Arms extended with upright palms, rhythmically place one palm in the other, alternating top palm and gradually lifting the motion to the sky, with eyes on your hands)
> Forgive Us as We Forgive Others
> > (Left arm extended out and slightly up while bending right arm at elbow and striking breast over the heart three times)
> Deliver Us from Evil
> > (Both arms extending from the shoulders over the head with head looking upward, and then arms brought down and crossed over the chest with head bowed)

## ☀ Prayer

Abba, with gratitude I receive your unconditional love and offer you my own in return. I unite myself with the prayer of Jesus and seek to create a cloister in my heart where I can come to know myself as you know me, to understand your will for my life and to receive the courage to fulfill it through service to the needs of the world around me. Like Jesus, my prayers rise like incense in your sight. Amen.

## STEP SIX

# See
# the
# Good

Don't judge, so that you won't be judged. For with whatever judgment you judge, you will be judged; and with whatever measure you measure, it will be measured to you. Why do you see the speck that is in your brother's eye, but don't consider the beam that is in your own eye? Or how will you tell your brother, "Let me remove the speck from your eye"; and behold the beam is in your own eye? You hypocrite! First remove the beam out of your own eye, and then you can see clearly to remove the speck out of your brother's eye.

Matthew 7:1–5

## Imagine and Reflect

The good is all around us.
It is our sight
That fails.

Good and evil abide
Side by side,
And God's mercy falls
On both.

I cannot separate the Holy One
From those he has placed in this world
To accompany me.

I cannot cling to Christ
And ignore others;
For in clinging to him
I am forever bonded to them.

## Remove the Beam

In this sixth step along our spiritual path of discipleship, we unwrap Jesus' teaching about judgment. He seems to hold up a mirror and say, "Before you issue a judgment, decide if it is one you would want me to make on you." There is no one I know that enjoys being the focus of someone else's critical judgment. Most of the conflict in the world, in our Church, in our families, and within our own hearts resides in judgments that are made either without substantial information to uphold them or without the complementary desire to seek understanding of the person or situation under judgment. Such judgments wither our sense of what is possible. They stunt our ability to see ourselves with God's eyes.

On the other hand, we have all benefitted when someone offered us a benign judgment, one that affirmed our goodness and looked beyond our obvious flaws to what was good in us. That type of judgment fosters love and a desire to continue to radiate good even as it affirms us. It uplifts us and changes not only how we see ourselves but also our capacity to "pass it forward" and to see good in others.

As we reflect on step six, we let go of the nets of preconceived notions, past experiences, and current events in order to learn how to judge by kingdom standards. We surrender our quick judgments as we intentionally try to see the good in ourselves or others. Isn't this what Jesus showed us as he bypassed the external circumstances of those he met, looking instead into their hearts? He demonstrated what God does when God looks at us. This is what he tried to teach the disciples who walked with him—that God, who is good, is present in all people and all situations if we only have eyes to see. It is we who need to learn how to see rightly. We can all find what is wrong, but can we see the good?

## Entering the Scripture Story: Is Anyone a Worthy Judge?

Jesus' teaching on judgment is found within the many individual lessons following the Beatitudes. We met the first Beatitude on being the poor in spirit in step two, where Jesus introduced us to his paradoxical lessons on the source of real blessing. Each scriptural teaching after that seems designed to expand on those eight singular blessings so that his disciples (then and now) receive clear guidance on what we can expect if we follow the Way. In these teachings, Jesus focused on specific instances in our lives: anger, adultery, love of enemies, almsgiving, prayer, fasting, worry, judging others, the golden rule, and so forth. It's almost like having an "all occasion directory" the disciples can refer to when they go off to tell his story to others, to make new disciples.

Wedged into the middle of this list of teachings is one suggesting that we judge others based on changing the way we see them. This requires us to ask ourselves to look within at what colors our judgment, to determine the health of our internal sight, and to be reminded of who we are called to be in Christ. The teaching on judgment is an easy teaching to skip over, placed as it is between those two glorious behemoths of the Beatitudes and the golden rule. But what is most compelling is the fact that Jesus tells us that the way we judge others will be the measuring stick for how we will be judged by him; the criteria we use to measure another's worth, goodness, errors, or dignity will be the measure that is used on us. It's definitely not a teaching to take lightly.

Jesus offered this teaching in the midst of forming the character of his disciples. He doesn't seem to be looking for a generic, "seen one you've seen them all" kind of follower. He picks vivid personalities with varied backgrounds. We've already seen that they are ordinary, everyday people. We also know that they are not docile men and women who simply do what they are told, without questions or understanding. Jesus seems to choose people he can count on to develop kingdom attitudes, to understand the criteria God uses for judging and assessing, to think for themselves, and to make a free choice to follow him, willing to go all the way. He wants people who see others as God sees them—as beloved. It is this kind of people who make worthy judges because they are slow to render judgment and, when pressed, defer judgment to God.

The gospels bring only glimpses of the formative teaching Jesus gave his disciples, but in each case, his teaching pricks their conscience, asks hard questions, challenges "human nature," and invites the disciples to plug into their "divine nature" as they work to pass on to others Jesus' message of God's love and "seeing the good."

### Evaluate your evaluation

So many factors affect how we evaluate ourselves and others, and most of them are culturally conditioned. All factors are significant but seldom are the criteria on which we've learned to base our judgments, those that are most relevant in living our discipleship. The transition from making judgments based on our own histories to making judgments based on the teachings of our faith and our personal relationship with Christ isn't easy.

When I was a young girl, I lived in a part of the city dominated by one ethnic group. There were very few Italians in my part of town. Most of the time this wasn't an issue, but I have vivid recollections of those times when other children hurled ethnically charged words, heaved stones, and chased me home from school simply to show me that I was not valued. They judged me not by their experience of me at school or in the classroom but by what they heard in their homes or from others on the playground about "Eye-talyuns." They measured me by my lack of blond hair, blue eyes, and an ethnic genetic background that was dissimilar to theirs. My cultural conditioning told me to judge these other children and their parents as bigots, or mean, ignorant people. But my faith called me to see that "they know not what they do" and to move forward in attempting to establish relationships based on respect. Was it easy? No. Was it possible? Yes.

I can only hope that as they grew in wisdom, age, and grace their measures for determining a person's worth gave way to a deeper and more enhanced understanding that every human person has dignity and is worthy of respect. I can only hope that what we learned in the years of our Catholic education took root. I know it took root in me and shaped my passion for justice, openness to others, desire to create a welcoming environment for the stranger, and sadness whenever I realize that I have succumbed to the traps of my own imperfections.

But how do we form attitudes and choices that cause us to see the good in others rather than to cast judgment? How do we learn to walk in the footsteps of Jesus?

### Blessed . . . those who give others what they themselves want

Since most of the teachings in this section of the gospel we are considering are about practices or attitudes that were common in first-century Palestine, it's clear that Jesus drew on issues pertinent to the lives of ordinary people so that he could show them how to look at life through God's eyes. It's significant that Jesus' teaching on judging comes after the Beatitudes, with its positive list of what constitutes happiness for disciples, and is followed by a rule of life based on love, for it tells us that if we are to be blessed and happy, the type of judgment that counts is one based on love.

At face value this teaching on judgment in Matthew seems contradictory to John 9:39, "For judgment I came into the world, that those who do not see may see, and those who see may become blind." But on deeper reflection, they seem to clarify and complete each other. Both refer to how we see things and imply that seeing with God's eyes leads one to conversion, that sting associated with letting go of former ways of judging and claiming the power of compassion. Further, Jesus uses this teaching to offer us tips for our own transformation.

### Clear-sighted judgment

The first tip Jesus offers is that we need to be clear-sighted, to correct both our internal and external eyesight. He indicates that we can create a judgment based on what our eyes see or we can interpret those same images through insight, that wisdom that comes from relying on the truth God has "written" on our hearts and that is made explicit in the teachings of Jesus.

Now here is where it gets interesting. What is the measure that Jesus will use to judge and to bring about this new way of seeing? How do we grow more clear-sighted?

Many people in the developed world use criteria like economic status, education, personality, physical beauty, power or influence, effectiveness, and efficiency to make their judgments on worth. Jesus holds up a different template. He says, "Father, forgive them for they know not what they do." He extols those who exhibit humility, endurance in the face of hardship, faith, dependence on God, kindness, acceptance of others, self-esteem based on belief in God's abiding presence, respect for life, and forgiveness.

The judgment criteria Jesus sets for his disciples reverse so much of what we have been taught culturally. So, if we choose to see with God's eyes and understand with God's heart, then we should expect a certain level of discomfort.

## See through the lens of compassion

A second tip is that learning to see—to judge—with God's eyes depends on our ability to see *ourselves* with compassion. Seeing the beam in our own eyes from the perspective of compassion expands our ability to look at others with compassion as well.

We see this demonstrated in the story of the woman caught in adultery who is about to be stoned, according to the law. From outward appearances, she is in the wrong and deserves the consequences of her choices. However, in Jesus' "judgment" we see something else. He does not dismiss or ignore her sin, but as he looks on her with compassion and sees her fear, her vulnerability, and the dishonesty of the situation in which she finds herself, his judgment is transformed. She, the one abused, is to be stoned while those who would use her in a sinful way are allowed to cast the stones. Those guilty of the same sin are allowed to judge this woman and to decide her fate. Jesus sees what is not obvious to the eye but clear to the compassionate heart, and he offers her another chance. His judgment saves her life, causes the men to reevaluate their decision, and motivates all to refocus their lives on what is pleasing to God.

This is what happens whenever compassion is the compass that guides our judgment. This is what seeing with God's eyes looks like.

## What Does the Story Mean Today?

In a recent class I asked the question, "When, most recently, have you experienced a glimpse of the reign of God—a person, event, or situation that showed you that God was the most important person there and that God's rule was the rule of choice?" Many responded with excellent examples, but one respondent caught my attention when she said, "I can't remember having that kind of experience. I don't think I've ever glimpsed the reign of God in another person or place . . . but I have *seen* it in nature . . . in the beauty and order of nature." It struck me then that in order to experience God's kingdom, we have to be awake and alert to God's presence; we have to see it. And before we can *see* God's presence, we have to believe that all creation is imbued with it, including all human beings. This ability to see God's presence is the same quality that we need if we are to judge with compassion, in the style of God. God sees with the eyes of God's heart, which is love.

## Waking up to the reign of God

Being aware of God's kingdom and what God sees when he looks at our world and our lives takes vision, an ability to look beyond what is obvious to a deeper meaning. It takes being awake and not wandering through life in a semiconscious state. Jesus did this in the case of choosing and forming his disciples. In a sense, he *didn't* choose them. Rather, he presented himself to them and allowed them to choose to throw in their lot with him—to follow him. They had to be alert and awake to the possibilities and to see not just a man but someone worth following. They made the choice and acted on it. We are meant to do the same.

In step one, we learned that discipleship is always about replying to an invitation to follow the Lord; without this free-will ability, the decision to choose Jesus and the reign of God loses its meaning. When bystanders wanted to know about Jesus and what motivated his behaviors and choices, he said, "Come and see." He says that to us day in and day out, because the choice to follow Christ is not a onetime thing. It takes insight that goes beyond the immediate moment and the present situation.

Making the decision to follow Jesus is something that is presented to us in every real-life encounter we have. It is here that values laid out by Jesus bump up against our cultural formation and we are given the opportunity to see with God's eyes: when a coworker takes credit for our ideas; when our children fail to live up to their potential; when our neighbors treat us poorly or are unfriendly; when we see a hungry person seeking food; when our nation chooses violence in its search for peace; or when our church fails to live up to its own creed.

In contrast, we also are invited to see with God's eyes whenever we offer praise and thanksgiving for a beautiful sunrise or sunset, receive the gracious love of another, see the power of God in someone's healing; overcome temptation, participate in Eucharist, and are strengthened to service. The invitation to "come and see" is extended to us daily. All we have to do is to take off our blinders and say, "yes."

### Jesus' school of discipleship

John's gospel depicts two strategies in Jesus' school for disciples: The first twelve chapters of the gospel show Jesus' public ministry of instruction and healing that revealed him to all and invited them to choose to follow him. In the final eight chapters, Jesus gives precise instruction to those who have made the choice. This way of developing disciples corresponds to the natural way we choose our own companions: First we get to know the person and they come to know us; then we decide whether or not to associate with that person on a consistent basis—to become a friend. Becoming a friend is seldom an instantaneous process. It takes time.

As a disciple we not only associate with a person, Jesus, but also are befriended by him, and we place ourselves, our reputation, and our future on the line under this person's guidance. We don't have the luxury of a "Google search" to call up Jesus' recent words or activities, yet those who decide to turn their lives over to Jesus need some kind of guidance so that their choice comes from a life conversion, not a trend.

### Learn from the Bible and living witnesses

Learning about Jesus and being formed in discipleship relies on two primary sources: the Bible, especially the New Testament, and other disciples. The Bible is an ancient text, written in faith by loyal disciples who were trying to convince others to accept Jesus Christ and were inspired by God's vision of the world and human beings. For Christians, the New Testament is the basis of faith, moral teaching, and guidance in how to approach life in the manner of Jesus, who told us that he came not to abolish the law (Old Testament) but "to fulfill it."

The inspired witness of the scriptures brings comfort and discomfort; it affirms the good works that faith leads to and challenges decisions to place any person, ideology, organization, or attitude above that of God's rule in Jesus Christ. We can trust the scriptures to provide a "way of seeing" consistent with and adhering to the vision Jesus held out about the kingdom of God. We can trust that if we embrace the scriptures, they will equip us to become disciples and to live our spiritual destiny. If we judge (that is, see rightly, see the good) with the Gospel as our guide, we are assured that our judgments will receive the blessing that Jesus affirms.

Earlier, we recalled the story of the woman about to be stoned. Her accusers saw her through "the law," and also saw their freedom from the same rules that governed her life. They judged her, not with compassion, but with righteousness; not in mercy, but in hostility. Their judgment not only would have taken her life but also sent the message that she was not worth consideration, that her life was expendable. When Jesus entered the picture, the atmosphere changed, and so did the result. Instead of her sin, Jesus saw her need for forgiveness. Instead of their purity, Jesus saw in the men their sin. He looked with the eyes of God and acted on what he saw. He forgave the woman and revealed to the men their sin. He gave the woman the choice to "go and sin no more," and the men, the choice of how to respond—to walk away or to "cast the first stone."

Did the woman being stoned for adultery suddenly become pure? Did those who tried to stone her experience complete transformation of heart and mind? We do not know. We do know all received deeper insight into their own nature. He offered them the ability to see rightly, which allowed them to judge themselves and to choose the path of compassion rather than the way of violence. We do know that Jesus condemned neither the woman nor her attackers; instead, he set the measure by which they would measure, pointing out how a person apprenticed to God could live and gave them the chance to choose.

## The rush to judgment

If we continue to set our sights on the measurement held up by Jesus and revealed in the scriptures, we begin to grasp Jesus' guidance on how to "see."

Time and again Jesus reminds us that even those who sin the most remain worthy of God's love and forgiveness; even those who betray him can wear the mantle of discipleship and lead others on that path. For Jesus, it was not the "sin" of the moment that seemed to make the difference but what was in the heart and how people responded when their sins became apparent to them.

We all grew up being evaluated from the outside—is she polite enough, is he rugged enough, will they conform to the norms of the family, the neighborhood, and the Church? These judgments and imperfect "measurements" spell the difference between a secure and confident existence and defeat. But,

What if those who looked at you looked with the heart of Jesus?

What if those who called your name did so with respect and love?

What if the measurement of your worth was your existence, not your color, religion, or wealth?

What if the rush to judgment was based on the good you do,

The kind words you speak,
The sacrifices you make?
What if?

And what if you were able to see Jesus in the people at whom you looked?

What if you were able to find some good in those in whom you see the most egregious flaws?

What if each of us who bow our heads at the name of Jesus looked for the good and judged based on God's compassionate love?

 ## Questions

### for Reflection, Journaling, and Discussion

1. What is your experience of others' offering a good judgment on you? How does that compare to your own approach?

2. What cultural criteria for how to make judgments were passed on to you? In what ways are they supported or challenged by the teaching of Christ?

3. Have you ever been wrong in your judgment of another? How did you undo any harm your judgment may have caused?

4. The gospels show us a Jesus who looked for and found the good in others. In what ways do you follow this example? What do you do when you see a good quality, attitude, or behavior in another person?

5. By what measure do you judge yourself? Do you look at yourself with Christ's eyes and heart? What would

you see if you did? How might that affect your own clear-sightedness?

6.  As you reflect on the story of the woman about to be stoned, in what role do you see yourself, and what does this teaching of Jesus on judgment say to you?

## ✳ Journal Your Thoughts:
##  Look With the Heart

## A Ritual for Seeing the Good

Step six on the disciple's path begs us to learn a whole new way of measuring our own and others' worth. It encourages us to look at others with the heart of Christ and to use his measuring criteria to determine our approach.

As evidence of your mastery of this step of formation, try an experiment today or this week sometime:

With a notebook and pencil in hand, walk in a populated area of your town or at work. As you move through the day, focus your attention on those around you. You may simply observe them (e.g., you're in line at the post office) or you may be interacting with them. In any case, jot down the good you see being done, any kind words you notice or a manner of presence that is gentle, welcoming, soothing, or helpful. When you see something, jot it down and then go to that person and affirm that quality or action, saying (in your own words), "I noticed that you were so gentle with your little girl, and it reminded me that the kingdom of God is built by actions like that. Thank you."

Not only will you be surprised by what your action initiates, but you'll notice that paying attention to the good in others leaves no time to focus on or judge them for anything negative.

At night, review your list of notations (and try to make this a habit of daily action and not just a onetime thing), using the prayer below to ask the Lord to guide your own actions and words.

## ※ Prayer

Lord Jesus, on the final day you will judge me face to face. You will show me how well I lived as your disciple—how much I learned from you and put into practice with others. So many around me live gentle lives without realizing it is in imitation of you. Thank you for their inspiring witness and grant me the grace to live a conscious life—aware that I am learning from you, who are meek and humble of heart. Continue, Lord, to give me clear insight that I might see with God's eyes, as you do, and judge with compassion. May my walk through life leave an aroma of your presence wherever I go. Amen.

## STEP SEVEN

# Heal
# All You Meet

When he entered Capernaum, a centurion came to him, appealing to him and saying: "Lord, my servant is lying at home paralyzed, in terrible distress." And he said to him, "I will come and cure him." The centurion answered, "Lord I am not worthy to have you come under my roof; but only speak the word, and my servant will be healed. For I also am a man under authority, with soldiers under me; and I say to one, 'Go,' and he goes and to another, 'Come,' and he comes and to my slave, 'Do this,' and the slave does it." When Jesus heard him, he was amazed and said to those who followed him . . . "Go let it be done to you according to your faith."

Matthew 8:5–10, 13

## Imagine and Reflect

When the sun's rays break into shafts of light
We stand in awed wonder;
Cocoons open, freeing their occupants for flight,
And we are transfixed.
In the beauty and wonder of nature
Our hearts expand.
Hosanna, we cry,
All hail the Prince of Light.

When all is well
And the world circles in its orderly orbit,
The ego swells with pride
Imagining that this is what our hands have wrought,
Forgetful of the creative power
That stirs the universe

But when the heart shatters,
And faith hangs in limbo,
When the wounds of life seem insurmountable,
Then our leprous hands cling
To the hope buried within our deepest being,
Crying for what our souls long to receive.

A Savior,
Then, we seek a healing Savior.

# I Will Come and Cure ·

The first thing we notice in the seventh step of our disciple's
journey is that we add the verb "heal" to the list of qualities we
are trying to incorporate into our lives. We also notice that the
healing Jesus offers is freely given to anyone who asks. Earlier
in the scriptures we saw it given to a leper and now to a Roman

centurion. We also notice that Jesus is utterly self-confident in his power to heal, saying, "I will come and cure"—what a startling statement: not "I'll come and assess the situation" and not "I'll come as soon as I can and see what can be done," but rather "I will come and cure." Jesus knows who he is and what he is about, and his knowledge is rooted in his deep understanding of who God is and how God works in and through him. Finally, we notice that it is not just the centurion's servant who experiences healing: The centurion, the crowd, and one imagines, the disciples, are all moved to heal that twinge of disbelief they may have had in who Jesus was. They are forced by the witness of their own eyes and ears to open themselves to the power of God at work in Jesus.

In this chapter, we reflect not only on Jesus' desire and ability to heal as found in the story of the centurion, but also on how the actions and faith of the centurion are examples for us as we continue to learn how to follow Christ as his witness and agent of healing. Remember, Jesus told his disciples, "I tell you the truth, anyone who has faith in me will do what I have been doing. He will do even greater things than these, because I am going to the Father" (Jn 14:12).

The healing of the centurion's servant follows several stories and teaching Jesus offered to the crowds who followed him. Two that stand out immediately prior to this one are the Sermon on the Mount and the leper seeking healing. Combined, they point out important elements in Jesus' ministry: an understanding of his authority and of his power to heal as well as a crystallization of our own call to heal.

As we look at authority and power in the light of the Gospel, and in their relationship to healing, our healing task as disciples takes on new meaning and relevance.

*Entering the Scripture Story:*
*The Authority of Jesus*

The scriptures tell us that when Jesus finished his teaching on the mount, he continued to move through Galilee breaking open the Beatitudes by speaking on particular related issues. We are told that "the crowds were astounded at his teaching for he taught them as one having authority, and not as their scribes" (Mt 7:28–29). This reference to authority is important because the centurion brings it up again in the primary scripture for this seventh step. Here we take a moment to examine what authority is and how the authority of Jesus is different from that of the scribes and related to healing.

Authority, defined as "rightful power," is subjective; it relies on an individual's perception of its rightness. On the other hand, power is defined as the ability to influence the outcome of events. Power may be rightly used power, incorrectly used power, or power exerted by sheer force and coercion. However we define them, power and authority are different but related. In Jesus, both live harmoniously and always produce positive results.

There are a number of different types of authority.

- One is associated with someone who has **power "over" us**, the ability to control us or set boundaries, like a teacher, parent, or government official. This authority can seem onerous and stifling at times, and there are often acts of rebellion to throw it off.

- Sometimes we experience the **"delegated" authority** of one who acts on someone else's behalf or on behalf of a group or organization, such as a press secretary deflecting questions about a person or firm's decisions and activities. The authority in question isn't their own but is witnessing to another's authority.

- Some **authority comes from proven expertise or knowledge** acquired in our professional lives. We become an expert and our expertise enhances our credibility and, thus, our authority.

- Authority, the ability to command or act on one's own behalf, is the rightful use of power as the ability to influence an outcome.

## How Is Authority and Power Understood in the Light of Faith?

Based on Matthew's description of the crowds comparing the authority and power of Jesus to that of their scribes, it seems that there must have been obvious differences, but what were they? The role of scribe has a long history in Judaism and, as found in the Old Testament, was generally understood as a record keeper. Over time, scribes took a more active role in the religious development of the people and became known as lawyers, even experts in the law. By the time of Jesus, the scribes were closely associated with the Pharisees (high priests), and together they added *their own* opinions and traditions to the actual law that God gave the people through Moses. In other words, scribes were not authors of the law—the law did not originate with them; rather, they wrote and taught *their own* interpretations of the Torah. They did not claim the teachings as their own; they did claim the authority to enforce their teaching. They had no right to exercise this power. *This is the first important point to understand. They exercised power over the people, through their laws and teachings, but they had no authority to exercise that kind of power.*

The Hebrew scriptures use concepts like "dominion" and "rule" to describe authority and portray God as the source of all authority. God shows his authority in a number of ways in the Old Testament: as the Creator and sustainer of all life; as One who has moral precedence; as the liberator of Israel—the One whose power is always used to free and not to oppress; and as the transcendent God, greater than all other gods and whose self-validating presence inspires awe and reverence. This God of Moses is the One who called forth Israel's leaders and prophets and in whose name miracles were wrought. *This is the second important point: God's authority resides in God's self; it does not come from someone else.*

In the New Testament, this sacred, self-validating authority resides in Jesus, who says, "All authority in heaven and on earth has been given to me" (Mt 28:18). While Jesus claims oneness with his Father, he also says that the Father is "One who is greater than me." He submits to the Father's authority in the garden and does not use his own authority to minimize his suffering. This effort of Jesus to show authority not as *power over* but as *power for*, and that desires a relationship of love, is one of the reasons Jesus and the scribes and Pharisees clashed so mightily. Where they would use their *acquired* authority to restrict, inhibit, and burden people, adding to their suffering, Jesus used his *self-validated* authority to point toward God's rule, to heal, to affirm, and to lift up. *This is a third important point: Power and authority should be used to alleviate suffering, not increase it.*

As the relationship between authority, power, and healing evolve, we see that Jesus exuded the kind of wisdom-authority lived by the ancient prophets. They understood that God spoke through them and that any power they had flowed from the power of God, the Great Liberator and Healer, who resided in them. Even the crowds realized how different his authority was from that which they usually experienced. Jesus, the greatest and last of all the prophets of Israel, took his authority one step further. He claimed it as intrinsic to his own person, which was in full communion with God.

The authority Jesus projected was the authority that has truth as its foundation. This truth is that Jesus had rightful power to influence the outcome of events. It came from within him and was not based on what others thought or did. The crowd's reaction demonstrates in a powerful way that Jesus was not trying to control them, nor was he acting as a delegate for another, nor was he simply sharing the wisdom of his experience or learning. Rather, Jesus was offering them the truth that he and God were one. He brings them the God of Moses and all the prophets, the "living" word of God, encased in his own person, and they recognize it when they hear and see it. He knew what he believed, not as one repeating the teaching of another, as the scribes did, but as one who originated the teaching and who epitomized the teaching. Jesus is the living authority of God; not only is his *teaching* truth, but also *he*, the Teacher, is "the Way, the Truth and the Life" (Jn 14:6).

This understanding of Jesus' authority and power is important to how we understand healing for three reasons: First, God's power always bring forth new life, healing, freedom, faith, peace, and a call to discipleship. Second, God's power creates healing and wholeness in those who receive it, which is meant to be shared. Finally, as those who follow Christ commit ourselves to carry on his mission in the world today, we commit also to use our baptismal authority and power to spread wholeness, healing, freedom, peace, joy, and new life wherever we go. The ability to heal is not a "gift" given to the few, but a mandate given to every member of the Body of Christ.

Knowing this connection is important as we examine Jesus' encounter with the centurion, who was a man of authority himself and became an unwitting witness to faith. Did he believe before this encounter, or was he just desperate for a cure? We don't know, but we do know he believed in Jesus "enough" to become a conduit for Jesus' healing power.

## Make me clean

Matthew immediately follows the story of the crowd's insight into Christ's authority and rightful use of power with a story that shifts the focus from Jesus as teacher to Jesus as healer, reminding us that Jesus' teaching authority is intimately linked to his power to heal. Matthew tells us that a leper approached Jesus on his knees and asked for healing (Mt 8:1–4). He says, "Lord, *if you choose*, you can make me clean." The telling phrase, "if you choose," implies that Jesus is not only capable of healing others but also has authority over himself and can determine how to use his power.

Lepers were first-century outcasts. They lived outside the community and were forbidden to come into contact with "clean" people, often having to ring a bell to announce their approach so that others could avoid them or risk becoming "unclean" themselves. Those with leprosy did not belong except to each other. So some very interesting dynamics occur in this passage that contrast with the centurion's story that follows it: The leper approaches Jesus, speaks to Jesus, and asks for help. This leper asks Jesus not just to take away his leprosy but also to make him "clean." He was ostracized from the community not just because of a disease but also because the society of the time believed that disease was a symptom of a deeper problem, sin. The leper wants to rejoin the community, to associate freely with others, and to belong. And he has the clear insight to see that Jesus has the power to bring him back in "touch" with others, to create a place for him among those who are well.

We know (as the leper could only hope when making his request) that Jesus does choose to heal him and also exhorts him not to tell others. Rather, Jesus suggests that the leper begin acting as others in the community would, to acknowledge the power of God and to offer a gift of gratitude for God's loving-kindness. Here we see Jesus acting on his own authority, choosing to heal not for his own benefit but in order to give glory to God, not based on his own will but in order to witness to what God's will is, "the will of the one who sent me" (Jn 5:30). He brings the leper to wholeness in body and in soul and gives him a new life in the community. That is the will of God. The leper's healing takes two forms: physical and spiritual. It affects the faith of the leper as well as the faith of the crowd and the disciples.

### Only say the word

Finally, we come back to the centurion's plea to heal his servant. The centurion, unlike the leper, understands the luxury of having authority, as in rightful power over others. He has a responsible job commanding up to one hundred men within a Roman legion. The centurion is a public figure, an employee of the state, yet he approaches an itinerant Jewish rabbi, a carpenter from a disregarded region, and asks for healing for a member of his household. That, in itself, seems a miracle. It's comparable to the commander of the US forces in the Pacific going to a traveling evangelist to enlist his help with a maid's debilitating disease. Something seems out of kilter with this picture.

But what this story confirms for us is that *those who seek healing* are empowered to ask for it when they have faith that God can provide it. The leper recognized the truth of Jesus' power, and so did the centurion. It was the authentic power of one in whom God resides. When Jesus assures the centurion that he will come and cure, the centurion is overwhelmed. Perhaps he thought Jesus would rebuff him because he was not a Jew, or maybe he thought Jesus would send a surrogate. Instead, Jesus honors the request with his own presence and assurance. We imagine the centurion thinking, "I'm not worthy of such a magnanimous gesture. I've seen what you can do and I believe it comes from a powerful place. I'm not a Jew. I'm viewed as an outcast and oppressor by your people, but I know the truth when I see it. You are a holy man of God with power that you use to help others. I believe you can heal, if you choose to do so."

Not only does Jesus choose to heal the centurion's servant, but also he heaps accolades on the centurion's faith, which he implies was the real motivator for the healing. Was it faith as a Jew knew faith, in the one God? No, the centurion's faith was in Jesus and what Jesus could do. That is the marvel of this story and our seventh step. This gentile recognized authentic authority, the kind that originates in God, and he saw this authoritative power residing in Jesus. His faith brought trust that, even though he was not worthy to receive what he requested, Jesus would still accomplish the healing if he believed it was right to do so. His faith in Jesus prompted the healing, and the healing enriched his faith.

## What Does the Story Mean Today?

Each of us has lived the meaning of these stories at one time or another. Like the centurion, we've claimed authority over our children or employees and felt distress and a desire to find healing for sick family and friends; like the leper, we've experienced illness or disease ourselves and cried out for God's mercy and healing. We've placed our faith and trust in our implicit understanding of Christ's rightful power to heal us with God's own healing. We have all experienced times of isolation, suffering, doubt, fear, and yearning for wholeness and new life, and often on our knees, we've come to Christ.

What we don't always do is recognize that healing comes in many forms and that we, too, are empowered to be channels of God healing. Exercising healing is one of the steps we must take if our following of Christ is to change our lives, the lives of others, and life of the world. The healing we offer to others will be based on faith in Christ and in God's desire to work through us to accomplish the mission of Christ in our times.

What follows are guidelines for navigating our invitation to claim our authority to heal. "Then Jesus summoned his twelve disciples and gave them authority over unclean spirits, to cast them out, and to cure every disease and every sickness" (Mt 10:1).

## Seek the truth

What is truth? This is one of the most significant questions of the Bible. It was what Pilate asked as he handed Jesus over to be crucified, in response to Jesus, who said, "I have come into the world *to testify to the truth*" (Jn 18:37).

History reveals that Pilate's question is still relevant. Some say truth is subjective, whatever our opinions determine; others believe truth is a product of consensus based on culture; and still others deny that truth can even exist. The scriptures tell us that truth is the self-expression of God and is revealed in all that is consistent with the mind, will, character, glory, and being of God. It also teaches that reality is what it is because God made it so from the beginning, as the author, source, and final judge of all truth.

The Old Testament refers to God as the "God of truth" (Dt 32:4; Ps 31:5; Is 65:16), making it clear that all truth must be defined in terms of God and God's original vision. In the New Testament, Jesus said of himself, "I am . . . the truth" (Jn 14:6), knowing full well what the Jews believed about God as truth. This is yet another sign of his authority, power, and oneness with God. And in knowing "the Truth" of God's creative vision, Jesus exercises his power to heal. Jesus is truth "in the flesh," the perfect expression of God, "the brightness of God's glory and the express image of His person" (Heb 1:3).

So this first guideline for our own ministry of healing is to look at others, situations, events, and circumstances through the lens of God's truth, expressed in Jesus; that is, God is Love and Love desires wholeness, harmony and peace, freedom, love, forgiveness, healing, and fruitfulness for all creation. Look for the lack of that truth in what is hurting and broken and you find that which needs healing.

### Recognize the cry of the broken

In our everyday lives, the need for the healing presence of Christ in the face of pain, alienation, fear, and death is everywhere. Jesus did not manufacture the healing needs of the people of his times. Rather, he responded, on an individual basis, to those who asked for healing as well as to those who could not yet express their own need.

If we as maturing disciples want to heal with Christ's authority, then we need to cultivate our ability to recognize the need for healing and, then, accept that disciples of Jesus are called to be instruments of God's healing. That twofold process requires that we relinquish our control by taking the focus off of ourselves and seeing the needs of others through the lens of God's truth. This outward-leaning perspective allows for authentic humility to emerge. In order to see the truth that needs healing, we cannot be the center of the universe, blinded by our own needs. When we do this, we also acknowledge that we can't "fix" things on our own. Instead, we have faith in the truth that it is God who heals in the ways God knows we need. And because of Jesus, we know that God chooses to come and cure.

The need for healing starts in naming our own brokenness, acknowledging that our own hearts often bear the scars of broken relationships, ignored or delayed dreams, abuse in many forms, anger and bitterness, rejection, and so much more. Too often the joy that life should evoke is smothered in an unhealed past that creates a need for our own healed present. We allow the power of God to heal us when, like Jesus in the garden, we fall to our knees in prayer and place our hope in the God who loves us, accepting that God's love wants what is best for us and will journey with us in each and every facet of our lives. This surrender, in trust and faith, gives us the power and the strength not just to endure but also to bring forth new life.

Outside of ourselves we have only to look at our family members and friends to see the next level of healing need. Who among us does not have a sibling, parent, extended relation, or friend who is underemployed, divorced, addicted, struggling to cope, ill, in jail, flunking out of school, or otherwise not whole and fully responsive to the blessings God holds out generously? Here is a ripe field in need of healing, and it was perhaps in this spirit that Jesus turned Mary over to John's care as Mary wept at the foot of the Cross. So often with family and friends, the healing response isn't an answer but an embrace. It isn't a solution but a readiness to listen without condemnation or conditions. Healing in these instances looks like presence, like an offer of prayers, and like a willingness to be a companion on the road to wholeness.

Beyond the intimacy of family and friends, we have only to look at our living and work environments to be bombarded with healing needs. Here we find employers whose desire for profits may override their concern for the good of their employees, or those who take advantage of immigrants, the disabled, or minorities, including women, and choose not to pay them fair and equal wages, to deny them health benefits, to use unethical business practices, or to provide unsafe work conditions. There also are employees in need of healing, who fail to offer a fair day's labor, cheat their employer, or create work environments filled with fear and intimidation. Disciples look beyond the visible brokenness of the workplace to the face of the missing truth of God's love for each person and the dignity with which each person is endowed. We heal here by treating all with respect; by calling into question that which denigrates anyone; and by witnessing to what is true through our own practices, words, and choices.

Don't forget about our Church family. Just because people of faith proclaim belief in God doesn't mean we do not bear the same marks of brokenness as others. The good news of God's love has been compromised in the hearts of many over the years, not only by the inconsistent ways in which God's people live the Gospel but also by the sins, mistakes, and omissions of Church leaders that have weakened their authority and credibility. Others look at us skeptically because they do not see in our actions what we proclaim with our lips. Jesus had harsh things to say to the Pharisees and high priests of his day because their exercise of authority and power did not alleviate the suffering of their people. Yet he welcomed the high priest Nicodemus who humbly showed his own need for conversion and sought out Jesus in order to be reconciled to the truth. We can be healers within our communities of faith every time we forgive the failings of our brothers and sisters and step forward in faith to offer our service on their behalf. We also heal when we do not sidestep the truth of a situation but bring false witness of the faith into the light and call for each person to stand up for the truth of the Gospel. In the Catholic tradition, we celebrate the sinner's claim on forgiveness as a sacrament, raising the ordinary to the divine.

Finally, our nation and our world are in need of healing. The individualism, violence, and greed that permeate our lives as citizens of the world have reached a crescendo bordering on cacophony. The beauty and harmony that characterized Eden, including the mutual respect and care that directed all interactions, seem submerged in competition for power and control over people and resources. God seems far from the conversation. Yet here, too, disciples can exercise our call to heal. It might take the form of letters to our elected representatives when the laws they wish to impose violate God's truth. It might be joining organizations that seek peace, conserve nature, or fight for the rights of those who are unjustly treated. It might be opening our hearts to other faiths and acting as an agent of reconciliation and hospitality within our local communities. The world is at our doorstep and provides us with ever new possibilities to heal that which is broken.

### Plead your need from a sincere heart

This third guideline asks us to look at our own lives and the lives of all others with whom we share this planet as opportunities for healing that should throw us to our knees to beg for it. As we do, we need to place our needs before Christ in a straightforward manner, rather than say with our lips what our hearts may not truly believe. How many people pray, "O Father, if it is your will, cure . . ." And then, when the person is not physically or mentally cured, they lose faith, they are dismayed and dejected, and they question whether God is listening. The prayer of a sincere heart seeks the healing that *God wants* and remembers that God always heals even when the evidence cannot be outwardly seen. The outcome will be the blessing we need, not necessarily the one we seek. Even death can be the great healing that our souls need and can be received as such if the prayer of our hearts is sincerely for God's will to be done and God's glory to be revealed.

## Leave the form of healing in God's hands

God can't work if we've already determined what form of heal-ing we will accept. If someone has cancer, then the only accept-able healing most of us want is a cure or permanent remission. And praying for that cure is certainly something we should do. But since the Lord sees the true source of our illness as well as the real healing we need, what if the healing the Lord sees we need is from a lack of forgiveness in our hearts, a refusal to heal an alienated relationship, a lack of faith in God's love, or an insincere promise to change our ways, rather than a physical healing? Leave the healing in the hands of the Healer.

As someone who does counseling and spiritual direction, I often spend time with people whose stated reason for seeking emotional or spiritual healing is quite different from the real needs we uncover as we work together in prayer and conversa-tion. So many times the brokenness or yearning for God that initiates our sessions is just the proverbial "tip of the iceberg." In honest exchange of truth, the real story is exposed, and if people are able to work through the truth of their lives, seek the healing power of God, and alter their perceptions of what is possible, the blessing of healing descends and the joy of new life is born.

In these instances, I have had the great gift of realizing that, in Christ's name, holding close the truth of God's unending love and mercy, all things are possible and I can be both an instrument and co-recipient of that healing revelation.

## Cultivate your faith

Faith is the fertile soil in which healing takes root and brings new life. It is a verb, a famous theologian once said. That means faith is not an intellectual exercise but a whole-person expe-rience of trust in that which cannot be clearly answered or revealed. Just as the farmer plants the seed in the soil, trusting that the sun, rain, and earthy nutrients will produce an abundant crop, we sow the gift of our faith in the soil of the teachings and witness of Jesus, in the memory of God's goodness throughout our lives, and in the grace of God's presence that never leaves us, trusting that it will grow and produce what we need to live lives of contentment. Just as the farmer is sometimes disappointed in the crop that is not what he wanted or expected, so too the realities of life may fall short of our expectations. But this is where the life of faith becomes real. As the farmer begins again with a new crop sowed with hope and trust, so we claim our faith and move forward relying on its Source to make all things well.

We can increase our faith, as the apostles' once desired, by practicing small acts of trust in ourselves, others, and God. We can practice the spiritual discipline of surrendering to God rather than trying to control every facet of our lives. We can end each day by praying prayers of gratitude for the small and large blessings we have received. The accumulation of these disciplines creates in us a capacity for an active faith that is spontaneous, alive, focused, and accessible so that when difficulties come and sorrow appears, we are able to dig deep into the soil of this faith and find there the ongoing source of life.

This kind of mature faith is essential to our ability to believe in God as healer and in ourselves as instruments of God's healing.

## Heal all you meet

This final guideline reminds us that as Christ's disciples we are on a mission, empowered by our baptism, to perform the works of Christ who gave us authority to do what he did: teach, preach, heal, forgive, feed hunger of every type, and bring life to the dying. Jesus shared his own authority with us and then sent us "into the whole world."

It's challenging to live in a world with constant news of violence and doubt, yet reach out with healing. We may want to ignore the daily news that focuses on what is broken, rather than *become* the "good" news that the world so needs. Ironically, we already carry within us the good news that can heal the planet and every living being on it. The healing truth is that every person is formed in the image and likeness of God with all the virtues and power that involves. As disciples, we need to live into that image, to believe the truth of that good news, to carry that truth into the face of what is broken, and to proclaim without hesitation to all who have ears to hear and eyes to see that message God sent so long ago, "This is my beloved."

If Jesus looked at the leper, the outcasts, and the marginalized and simply saw yet one more infringement upon his space, time, and energy, instead of a child of God and brother or sister for whom God wanted wholeness, he would easily have walked away without offering healing. He did not look at life this way. He certainly did not look at those seeking healing in this way.

If Jesus climbed the mountain where he preached the secrets of living a blessed life only to offer a "feel-good" ideology proven to make him popular instead of preaching the truth of God's kingdom, which often contradicts the prevailing social wisdom, he probably would have walked down the mountain as just another new rabbi with his own opinions and ideas. He did not.

If Jesus had looked at our centurion only as a man of war, oppression, and brutality and missed his authentic expression of faith and his desire to help another, he could have excused himself from helping "the enemy" and pleaded fatigue. He did not.

In each case, healing bubbled up far and beyond what was requested, healing not only bodies but also human spirits and fledgling faith in the truth of who our God is. Those who were healed became disciples. We are disciples who need healing and are invited to ask for healing from a God just waiting to fulfill our request. Even more, we are disciples who are given the power to offer that same healing, in Christ's name, to all we meet.

Look around. Where do you see the need for a healing Savior? How can you, relying on the truth of God's love and mercy and on the authority of your life in Christ, bring healing to your family, your neighborhood, your church, and your world?

## ☀ Questions
### for Reflection, Journaling, and Discussion

1. In whose authority do you place your trust? Who has the power to command your attention, to motivate your decisions? Make a list of the truths to which you give your life and the authors of each truth.

2. Which of those who asked for healing, the leper or centurion, most represents your own approach to Jesus? Do you approach Jesus without fear? Are you clear in how you ask for healing? Do you believe, truly, that Jesus can and will heal?

3. How is your faith affected by your prayer? How is your ability to be a healing presence affected by your faith?

4. If you feel reluctant to ask for healing, what holds you back? Is this perhaps the first healing that needs to take place?

5. Would you say you try to be a healing presence in the world? Describe the last time you realized that God acted through something you said or did to provide an experience of healing in mind, body, or spirit for someone else. Did you give God the glory?

## ☀ Journal Your Thoughts: Seek Healing

### A Ritual for Healing

In your journal or another place to which you refer often,

- Make a list of those people, places, or situations close to you that need healing. Like the centurion, be sensitive to the needs of others and determine what you can do to be an agent of their healing. Name the healing(s) you recognize is needed. Determine a plan for action on behalf of at least one on your list.
- Continue the list, with those areas within your own life that are broken: health, relationships, faith, and so on. Imitating the leper's humility, kneel and acknowledge your need for healing as you place your personal list in the Bible or on your prayer altar/space.
- Continuing to kneel, place your hand on the Bible and the list as you pray the closing prayer.

## ☀ A Prayer
### for Healing

Jesus, if you choose, you can heal me. Choose to heal me, Lord, in all the ways you know I need. I believe, I surrender, and I await in confidence the power of your love—without reservation, without determining the time, place, or form. Say but the word. Heal me even as I sing your praises to the ends of the earth. Amen.

**STEP EIGHT**

# Be Not Afraid

Immediately Jesus made the disciples get into the boat and go on ahead to the other side, while he dismissed the crowds. And after he had dismissed the crowds, he went up the mountain by himself to pray. When evening came, he was there alone, but by this time the boat, battered by the waves, was far from the land, for the wind was against them. And early in the morning he came walking toward them on the sea. But when the disciples saw him walking on the sea, they were terrified, saying, "It is a ghost!" And they cried out in fear. But immediately Jesus spoke to them and said, "Take heart, it is I; do not be afraid." Peter answered him, "Lord, if it is you, command me to come to you on the water." He said, "Come." So Peter got out of the boat, started walking on the water, and came toward Jesus. But when he noticed the strong wind, he became frightened, and beginning to sink, he cried out, "Lord, save me!" Jesus immediately reached out his hand and caught him, saying to him, "You of little faith, why did you doubt?" When they got into the boat, the wind ceased. And those in the boat worshiped him.

Matthew 14:22–33

133

## Imagine and Reflect

The boat rocks
Waves swell and crash
The wind sweeps down from the mountain
As night sets like an inkblot.
They are alone
And afraid.
Into the midst of their fear
Comes a figure
Walking toward them,
Their Lord
Their Savior.
When Jesus speaks, "It is I," to the heart
The disciple's seek the shelter of his love,
Awed by the reassurance of his protective embrace,
Drenched in grace-filled deliverance,
Without fear.

## Be Not Afraid

Our final step on the disciple's path addresses the obstacle of fear, as we hear the words of Jesus, "Take heart. It is I, do not be afraid." The most profound anthem of a disciple's spiritual life is found in Jesus' admonition to be fearless. *Be not afraid* is the most repeated message of Jesus in the gospels, even more than the command to love.

Why did Jesus make this his most often repeated message? What is there about human fear that capsizes our efforts to recognize Christ's presence and to place our trust in him? How can we put aside our natural fears so that Christ's Spirit can guide our steps and decisions? These are the questions we explore in this chapter. The answers can be summarized in our last verb, "trust." It is trust that shapes the beginning and the end of our disciple's path and accompanies us at each step of the way.

## Entering the Scripture Story: Naming and Overcoming Fear

Amid Jesus' numerous calls to fearlessness, the story of the boat ride on the Sea of Galilee is brilliantly gripping and one of my favorite passages. The Sea of Galilee, also known as Lake Kinneret or Lake Tiberius, is the largest freshwater lake in Israel, the lowest freshwater lake on earth, and the second-lowest lake in the world after the Dead Sea, which is saltwater. It's a dazzling sight, especially when the sun is glinting off its surface. In Jesus' time, the Sea of Galilee already hosted a thriving fishing colony with hundreds of boats regularly working its waters. Its position in a rift valley surrounded by hills makes it susceptible to sudden violent storms and a constantly changing natural character.

The Sermon on the Mount took place on a hill overlooking this lake. Jesus called Peter to fish "for men" and Andrew, James, and John to follow him on this lake. Many of Jesus' healing miracles happened near or on it. Often Jesus used the lake as a refuge from the crowds and as a travel route between Judea and Galilee. Much of Jesus' Galilean ministry involved this body of water, and it is the geographic area with which he is most familiar, having grown up in Nazareth, not far away. This snapshot of the Sea of Galilee and the significance it played in Jesus' life offers us some perspective for our reflection on Jesus and his disciples after a tiring day.

They were in a place they knew well, comfortable in the welcoming environment of Galilee and the sea. Five thousand had been fed with a few loaves and fishes not far away, and the crowds of people, who still did not understand the purpose and message of Jesus, were eager to have such a man as their

King, the One who would not only overthrow the Romans but also restore them to a land of milk and honey rather than the impoverishment they now experienced. The energy and sheer size of the crowd made it imperative for Jesus to find a place of solitude and rest. He must have been drained, since the feeding of the five thousand was the culmination of his work that day, and not his only work. Jesus didn't even want his disciples around him, so he sent them ahead, by boat, to their next stop while he went, as seems his custom, to a mountaintop for prayer and restoration.

Try to imagine the disciples filled with astonishment and a sense of invincibility as they reveled in their Master's abilities and popularity. Their Teacher had accomplished something so spectacular in feeding the vast crowds from so few resources. No one had ever done such a thing. But he was tired and they, themselves, needed time to process the experience and to understand its meaning. Life was good, the sea was calm, and they were ready to be alone, together, to talk about the day's events. They set off, at Jesus' instruction, to cross the sea to Capernaum, on the north side, in order to prepare things for his arrival. It was dark, but they seem nonchalant at the danger of being on a vast sea at night. Perhaps it came from their pride in their own experience as seamen and the skills and knowledge that gave them. Before they set off, did they factor in their weariness? In their exhilaration after the feeding, did they notice their environment and what the clouds held? The scripture doesn't tell us. We do know that they set off without argument, blinded to danger by the task at hand.

It is in the hills of Golan that surround the lake that storms traditionally gather energy and sweep down onto the water. This night is no exception. Swirling winds and rain blanket the sea, the boat, and everything within its range. Imagine the rocking boat as the wind increases and water rushes in from all sides. As skilled as the men are, they experienced fear as they tried to keep their boat afloat in the dark storm. A storm is never a good time to be out on this lake, especially "at a considerable distance" from shore. To add to their peril and to heighten their fear, they notice an image moving over the water toward them. Matthew tells us that they think it is a ghost, so in the cloud-covered moonlight, there must have been some kind of blurred image or aura. Fear built its home within them, and it had nothing to do with their experience of the churning sea.

### Courage

The scene is set. We see the disciples in the middle of the lake, in the midst of darkness. Scriptural *darkness* means more than a lack of physical light. It implies danger or evil. We see their small boat, the waves building, and the water lapping over the sides. We feel the change of temperature and the rocking motion. We hear their calls to each other with directions for actions that need to be taken. Perhaps we even hear their prayers. Visibility is minimal, and forward progress is stalled. It isn't too much of a stretch to imagine every available man bailing water. Anyone who has ever been on a boat in such a situation will remember how the heart races and the adrenalin surges as the body tries everything possible to calm its fear while the mind searches anxiously for a safe solution.

Interestingly, the scriptures don't record the disciples' fear of the storm; instead, we learn "they were terrified" when they saw an apparition coming toward them. Initially, they did not know it was Jesus. As he approaches the boat, his greeting to them comes in three parts:

*Take courage (in some translations, take heart).*

*It is I.*

*Do not be afraid.*

Notice that Jesus doesn't simply greet them; he *tells* them to "take heart," that is, to find their courage. As we explored together earlier, we know that the heart, for the Jews, was the center of their whole personality, including intuition, feeling, emotion, spirit, courage, and everything else that made a person, a person; the heart was considered the vital and essential core of a human being, their essence. And here is Jesus telling the disciples to look into their hearts and to find there the cheer, spirit, courage, and inspiration they had just a few hours before at the feeding of the five thousand. He tells them to go to their core and stand fast in all that makes them who they are as his followers and disciples, including their growing understanding that he is, indeed, the Christ.

And yet, we know that, when fear is great, it takes more than a command to conquer it. In this case, the disciples are less comforted by his call to take heart than terrified by his next words. Jesus tells them that they are able to take heart and find courage there because "It is I," a term that in the Greek, *ego eimi*, is also translated, "I am." For Jews, this was the sacred name of God. Surely the disciples immediately remembered Moses and the burning bush. No wonder they were terrified! Here is an apparition that sounds like Jesus, in whose presence they normally experience calm and courage, yet the apparition identifies himself in the same language they use for God. Was this a ghost? Was it Yahweh, come to take their lives? Or was this Jesus? Fear engulfed them. They did not recognize Jesus in this powerful apparition, nor did it occur to them that he would know of their danger and come to be with them. They didn't expect his help, so when it came, they weren't able to recognize it. Seeing their fear, he adds his third greeting, "Do not be afraid."

## Keep your eyes on Jesus

Matthew tells us that Peter tests his perception that the apparition is Jesus by asking to be allowed to walk to Jesus over the water. Jesus bids him come. Miraculously, Peter is able to step out of the boat and to walk on the water to Jesus. As the story describes, when Peter keeps his eyes on Christ, he is safe and moves forward. When he removes his eyes from Jesus and focuses instead on the danger of his situation, he sinks into the water and must cry out for Jesus to save him.

There are several elements in the chaos-fear-peace cycle of this story that will help us to understand the significance of the role of fear and trust in our spiritual journey. First, the disciples take for granted that their familiarity with their surroundings gives them control over the elements. They see themselves as strong, sea-smart men who have rowed across this sea hundreds of times and have fought off storms just as many. They are fearless because they acknowledge no force beyond their control. Their imaginations fail to conjure a situation that they cannot handle. They've left Jesus on shore thinking they have no need of his presence in this environment they know so well. The foolishness of their self-delusion and pride grows apparent when the storm threatens to end their lives. It is when they are afraid that they look beyond themselves for help. I recognize myself in this attitude. I've been guilty of that kind of pride that doesn't really think about the need for God when all is going well.

The second phase of the cycle rests on failing to recognize Jesus' love and desire to be with them, to protect them from themselves and all that is harmful. Even though he went off by himself to pray, Jesus did not forget about them or fail to recognize that they were in danger when the weather changed. He came to them, not because they called out to him—he was already on the way—but because he already knew their need for him before they asked. They see Jesus walking on the water toward them—coming to their rescue—but they feel terror rather than awe. Failing in recognition, they think he is a ghost, some "thing" not some "one" with whom they have a love relationship, whose gifts of healing they have witnessed and received, and in whom they have found a calling beyond the sea. They think their knowledge of him determines who he is. And now, when he is most present to them, when they cannot control their perceptions of him, they fear him. I found this true of my own journey at times. I try to place God in a box of my own making and, usually without realizing it, place boundaries around what God can and should accomplish. Like the psalmists, at times I want God to strike down my enemies and save me from all my foes. I want God to be on "my" side, and when life doesn't fit that expectation, I don't recognize that God is still present calling me to come across the water of fear to safety.

Finally, the disciples, exemplified by Peter, charge out onto the water, goading Jesus to use his power to prove who he is. Because Peter is impetuous and walking not in faith and trust in Jesus but in fear for his life, he takes his eyes off Jesus and focuses instead on his problem. The faith that originally spurred him to surrender his nets in order to follow Jesus, flounders when he allows his problems to be more powerful than trust in Jesus' saving presence. Here too I see the spiritual cycle of my own life. When I stay focused on Christ, I have inner peace regardless of the outward turmoil. When I try to live life on my own terms and forget why I said "yes" to Christ in the first place, I stumble.

## What Does the Story Mean Today?

There are some obvious parallels between the gospel story of Jesus and his disciples on the Sea of Galilee and our own struggles to trust the Lord before and beyond all others. I consider myself a deeply committed follower of Christ, someone who has nourished a rich relationship with Christ all of my life. Yet, I remember several significant times when fear threatened to overwhelm me. One, in particular, stands out. I was the sole breadwinner for my family, which at that time consisted of me, my husband, and my mother, whom I was caring for in the midst of her descent into Alzheimer's disease. It had been five years since my husband's traumatic brain injury, and though he functioned on his own, he was unable to accomplish many normal tasks or to work. Out of nowhere I lost my job of almost twenty-five years, including all my benefits. I was far too young for any kind of assistance. I was terrified. My field of theology did not easily translate into a paying job, especially where I lived. I indulged in worry, anxiety over how we would survive, and anger over the injustice of my situation. I argued, cajoled, and blamed the Lord for letting us down. Mostly, in my fear, I forgot about God's generous care in the past. I was blind to God's presence with me even in my struggle. I lost confidence in God's providence. I began to think that everything I had was a result of my own efforts and that the future depended on my efforts alone. I felt lost; my boat was swamped, and I was drowning.

Into the midst of this situation that seemed about to overwhelm me, the Lord gradually appeared. At first, even though I prayed daily, Christ seemed a distant memory. I could not grasp that God held me in the divine palm. Gradually, as I continued to pray, I experienced Christ as in a blur, beckoning with outstretched arm. In my times of quiet, I heard a repeated refrain, "trust, only trust." And I did. As that trust that God would not abandon me but would give me everything I needed to care for my family grew, so did my confidence in myself and my faith in Christ.

Like the disciples, we've all experienced times when we had a choice between allowing our fear to overcome us and trusting in God's presence, love, and power to heal and save us.

## Fear, Love, and Christ

It has been said that all of our responses in life come from either love or fear. I've learned that there are two things that make the vital difference and lessen fear's impact: awareness of what motivates us and our ability to choose how to respond to our feelings. Looking at each one, we see that awareness gives us the power of choice by showing us our options. Realizing our options bolsters our courage to choose an option consistent with our deepest values, hopes, and beliefs rather than with a fleeting emotion, no matter how powerful. We come to this awareness in quiet reflection as we take a step back from the immediacy of our fear and give ourselves time to review and understand the feeling as well as the consequences of acting on it.

It's clear that fear is a two-edged sword. It can catapult us to panic and flight or spur us to faith and action. The fear of life's difficult situations can only be overcome because our love of God and awe at his power is greater and casts it out. The psalmist cries, "I sought the Lord, and he answered me, and delivered me from all my fears" (Ps 34:9). God's deliverance is grace that sustains us in mercy and kindness in spite of our fears and leads us to spiritual maturity and wisdom—the ability to make choices based on God's everlasting love, not on evil's fleeting fear.

The disciples of the early Church knew this as they faced the brutality of gladiators and the savage attacks of animals. Each generation of disciples since has faced and questioned whether evil would triumph over God's goodness. Each age has learned that God reigns in spite of illness, tragedy, war, famine, and human sinfulness. What makes our age different is the rapidity with which we learn of such horrors and the vast numbers of people affected by the decisions of a few. In other words, as the world shrinks, fear seems to increase as less and less decision making is in our own hands.

If our response to life flows from love, then the need for awareness is the same, but the options expand because they are already in line with our values since love is at the center of who we are, and when we love, we are closest to God. Love allows us to choose from our deepest selves—our souls. That makes our choice to love "in spite of" the forces of fear life giving and powerful, for the love in us comes from a divine source.

In 1 John 4:18, we read, "There is no fear in love, but perfect love casts out fear." Fear is conquered through love, for we cannot fear that which we love. In counseling, when a client fears a spouse, child, parent, or significant other, it is my first clue that love is not the foundation of that relationship, at least at this time. That's a lesson the disciples forgot as they clung to their sea-tossed boat. It's a lesson Peter forgot until he sank into the sea and experienced the saving grasp of Jesus' love. It's a lesson I forgot until one day a wonderful job offer in another state came my way and I was able to refuse it because it would uproot my husband and mother from the only place they knew and felt safe. By allowing my love for them to overcome my fear of financial ruin, I remembered that there had been other swamped boats and other fears over the years, but God's love was steadfast and gave me what I needed not just to survive but also to thrive. I kept my eyes on Jesus, and it felt like walking on water.

Fear rows its boat in darkness, stretching its bleakness across each horizon, blotting out the safe shore ahead, and drowning trust in a sea swell of terror.

Love is the fabric of our being. We are stitched from its unconditional Source. A divine spark lives in us, was enfleshed in Jesus, and yearns to walk on the water of our trust without reserve, as we step onto the shore of God's presence. Jesus is love incarnate. Holding fast to his loving hand leaves no room for fear. In his presence, the wind and the sea are calmed, and fear has no dwelling place.

## Final Thoughts

Surrender. Bless. Love. Give. Pray. See. Heal. Trust.

As we conclude our walk together along the disciple's path, I invite you to remember the steps we've taken so that together we may renew our commitment to walk them each day.

The first step we reflected on in deepening our discipleship was our need to surrender all that holds us back from committing our lives to Christ. With our commitment in hand, we take the second step of living as a blessing—finding happiness in values that are countercultural. This inner conversion strengthens us for the third step, loving our enemies with a love so radical it frees us for the fourth step, which is to give generously of ourselves, our time, and our treasure as we embrace all and see in their need, Christ. Our fifth step recognizes that in order to sustain such generosity of heart and vulnerable love we need prayer, and the only prayer that can change our hearts is the prayer of Jesus. Through practicing the prayer of Jesus, we are released for the sixth step, to see the good in others rather than their flaws and to encourage that good to flourish. As we seek the good we are alerted to the need for our seventh step, to heal all we meet. We recognize that in order to accomplish Christ's mission of healing, we ourselves need wholeness, and we are empowered to foster this wholeness in others. In the end, our eighth step fuels them all for it reminds us that our commitment to follow Christ and bring about God's reign has to be done with trust in God's care to protect us, Christ's example to accompany us, and the Spirit to guide us—to move from the head to the heart and into action. We're called to step out in faith and to leave fear behind, to take heart in Christ and to fear not.

May it be so for you.

 ## Questions

### for Reflection, Journaling, and Discussion

1. Describe a time when you experienced the chaos-fear-calm cycle in your own life. At what point did you recognize Jesus' presence? What happened?

2. What is your experience of the relationship between fear and love? Does love cast out fear?

3. Notice when you are seeking control of people or events in your life. Describe the fears that are encouraging this control. What role does faith play in your choices?

4. Name your greatest fear in stepping out as a disciple of Christ? Do you have a favorite scripture that helps you to combat this fear?

## Journal Your Thoughts:
### I Have Nothing to Fear

## A Ritual for Casting Out Fear

Place some small pieces of blank paper, a metal or fire-safe dish, matches, and a candle on your prayer table/space, in a quiet place. Light the candle. Bring yourself to a reflective, meditative state through deep breathing. When your inner self is calm,

- Name one thing or person of which/whom you are fearful.

- Write the name of your fear on a piece of paper.

- Symbolize letting go of attempts to control this fear by taking the paper to a safe metal dish and burning it, as you trust in that divine, powerful, and loving nature within you, your "soul life," for support in moving forward without this fear in your life.

- Repeat the prayer, "O God, I love you. With you at my side I have nothing to fear."

- Sit quietly with your eyes closed while you imagine yourself acting with the freedom that this release of fear brings. Picture the fear you have released, see it floating away into oblivion, and see yourself without it. Repeat your prayer as needed.

- Repeat this process for as many fears as you wish over how long a time as it takes.

- When you are ready, pray the prayer below.

## ※ Prayer

Sweet Jesus, you who overcame fear with love, fill my entire being with your loving presence so that all fear evaporates. Strengthen my resolve to live in love. Give me the wisdom to recognize the temptation to act in fear so that I may choose love instead. With you at my side, O Jesus, I have courage; I rejoice in your divine presence; and I am unafraid. Amen.

**Linda Perrone Rooney** is a pastoral theologian, hospital chaplain, clinical pastoral education supervisor, pastoral counselor, and spiritual director. She is also a well-known teacher and retreat leader, having offered and taught retreats across the country. Rooney is an expert in the formation of lay ecclesial ministers and permanent deacons as well as adult spiritual development. She is the founding director of the Center for Healing and Spirituality in Winter Haven, Florida—a "place of the heart" that works to bring about an integration of body, mind, and spirit through teaching, counseling, and spiritual engagement. Rooney is the author of several books and two video-based adult formation programs: *Called and Gifted* and the parish-based training series Ministry to the Sick and Elderly.

Founded in 1865, Ave Maria Press,
a ministry of the Congregation of
Holy Cross, is a Catholic publishing
company that serves the spiritual and
formative needs of the Church and its
schools, institutions, and ministers;
Christian individuals and families; and
others seeking spiritual nourishment.

For a complete listing of titles from

Ave Maria Press

Sorin Books

Forest of Peace

Christian Classics

visit www.avemariapress.com

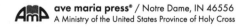 ave maria press® / Notre Dame, IN 46556
A Ministry of the United States Province of Holy Cross